STOMPING OUT FEAR

OUT FEAR

Neil T. AnDeRsOn
DaVe PaRk • RiCh MilleR

HARVEST HOUSE™ PUBLISHERS

EUGENE, OREGON

Cover by Left Coast Design, Portland, Oregon

Cover illustration by Krieg Barrie Illustration, Hoquiam, Washington

STOMPING OUT FEAR

Copyright © 2003 by Neil T. Anderson, Dave Park, and Rich Miller
Published by Harvest House Publishers
Eugene, Oregon 97402

Library of Congress Cataloging-in-Publication Data
Anderson, Neil T., 1942–
    Stomping out fear / Neil T. Anderson, Rich Miller, and Dave Park.
        p. cm.
Summary: Provides tools based on biblical teachings for dealing with baggage from the past and pressures in the present that can create fear, anxiety, isolation, and alienation.
Includes bibliographical references.
    ISBN 0-7369-0991-5 (pbk.)
    1. Peace of mind—Religious aspects—Christianity. 2. Fear—Religious aspects—Christianity. 3. Christian teenagers—Religious life. [1. Emotions—Religious aspects—Christianity. 2. Fear. 3. Trust in God. 4. Christian life.] I. Miller, Rich, 1954–   . II. Park, David, 1961–   . III. Title.
    BV4908.5 .A56 2003
    248.8'3—dc21   2002014924

Printed in the United States of America

03   04   05   06   07   08   09   10   11   / RDP-CF /   10   9   8   7   6   5   4   3   2   1

To the loving memory of Ira L. "Chub" Park

*My dad accepted Christ in 1996 at
a Promise Keepers event in Denver, Colorado,
and shook hands with Him on November 19, 2001.*

*Dad, I will miss your "Clark Gable" mustache,
Stetson hats, warm smile, and cowboy boots.
I am so proud to be your son and so thankful to God
that I was given a father like you. Dad, enjoy Jesus—
with Him there is no more fear, no more sorrow,
only God's awesome presence and peace.*

*If you're reading this dedication and you have
an unsaved loved one, don't lose hope. I prayed for
my dad for 19 years, and at the age of 67 he finally
received Christ as his personal Lord and Savior.*

—Dave

Acknowledgments

We want to thank the whole Harvest House team for another job well done and for the fine work of editing, designing, and marketing. You make writing books fun and rewarding. Special thanks to Paul Gossard.

Thank you to all the young people who courageously told us their stories—some of which are in this book, but all of which touched our hearts.

Finally, we want to thank our heavenly Father for calling us His children; Jesus Christ, who has set us free from fear; and the Holy Spirit, who leads us into all truth. We are indeed blessed with every spiritual blessing in Christ Jesus our Lord.

Contents

Foreword

by Josh D. McDowell

Traveling across the country and around the world, I have found that so many young people today are burdened with deep anxieties and fears in their lives. And with school violence, bombings, and terrorist attacks in the news, it's no wonder so many are living in fear. Many people are so overwhelmed that they can't even talk about what they are going through.

In their book *Stomping Out Fear*, Neil, Dave, and Rich clearly show that fear and anxiety come from a lack of understanding of who God is and who we are in Christ. They give rock-solid principles from the Word of God to point young people to Jesus, the One who can set us free.

Stomping Out Fear can help you learn who you really are in Christ and how you can be free from bondage and fear. I strongly encourage you to read this book and put the truth to work in your life. The apostle Paul says that "God has not given us a spirit of fear and timidity, but of power, love, and self-discipline" (2 Timothy 1:7 NLT). You belong to Jesus. A life free of fear can be yours!

Until the whole world hears,

Josh D. McDowell

A Note from the Authors

In relating true stories and testimonies throughout the book, we have changed names to protect individuals' identity and privacy.

For ease of reading we have not distinguished ourselves from each other in authorship or experiences, preferring to use "I" and "we" as opposed to "I (Dave)," "I (Rich)," or "I (Neil)." The only exceptions are illustrations referring to family.

The Fear Factor

FEAR. IT WAS THE FIRST NEGATIVE, ugly, really bad human emotion that humanity experienced after Adam and Eve sinned and fell away from God. "But the LORD God called to the man, 'Where are you?' He answered, 'I heard you in the garden, and I was afraid'" (Genesis 3:9-10 NIV).

We've all experienced fear—like when someone jumps out at us from around the corner and we about rocket out of our socks. That's healthy fear. To be honest, if you didn't jump, it would mean something was wrong with your reflexes.

That's not the kind of fear we are going to deal with in this book. Instead, we want to talk about what we call the "fear factor." With this kind of fear, you can't always put your finger on its source. For example, have you ever been so anxious over the uncertainties of the next day that you felt keyed up, tired, and irritable? You found it difficult to sleep, and you just couldn't relax because your mind was racing and your muscles were tense.

Or have you ever been paralyzed by fear to the point that you couldn't carry out your heart's desire? You knew what was right and you wanted to do the right thing, but some unknown fear kept you from doing it.

Or maybe you've had a sudden episode of intense fear that came out of the blue. You had shortness of breath and felt like you were being smothered. Your heart pounded, causing you to sweat profusely. You began to tremble, feeling unreal, like you were going crazy. You might have had chest pains and numbness or tingling in your hands and feet.

These are the symptoms of anxiety, fear, and panic, which cripple a large percentage of youth. You are experiencing the fear factor. Perhaps you can relate to the following cry for help:

> For as long as I can remember I have been plagued with fears and anxieties. I was raised in an abusive family and lived under the threat of even worse treatment if I ever told. In the bondage of fear, I decided to never tell anyone.
>
> I came home one evening and found everyone gone. I was gripped with fear and crawled under my bed. *Why aren't they home? Do they think I told someone? What's going to happen when they come back?* I could never enjoy the simple little things that accompany childhood.
>
> My anxieties and fears followed me wherever I went. I was too afraid to try out for anything where I could possibly fail, and I dreaded every exam. My stomach would tie up in knots from anxiety. I became a perfectionist who had to achieve—whatever the cost.
>
> This pattern of fear continued into my teenage years. I tried to accept Jesus twice, but I feared not being good enough. I feared the rejection and ridicule of others, so I tried to keep everyone happy. Even sleep offered no comfort. The nightmares I suffered as a result of the abuse in my childhood continued for many years.

> I know this is robbing me of the life I want to live, but I don't know what to do. I feel like I'm living two lives. On the outside I appear to be successful, but if people could see the condition of my soul, they would see only pain, anxiety, and fear. Can somebody help me? Can I help myself—or is this what life is supposed to be?

Fear and anxiety have surpassed depression and alcoholism as the number-one mental-health problem in America. And few of your friends will openly admit to their fears and anxieties. Most suffer through these experiences alone. Family and friends are often not aware of other people's private nightmares, so they can't understand why anxious people don't just "get with it." Perhaps you can relate to one or more of the symptoms we've presented, or perhaps you are trying to help someone else who can.

Are such mental, physical, and emotional reactions to life wrong? Shouldn't we be concerned about things we care about, and shouldn't we fear those things that threaten our lives? Wouldn't *anybody* panic if a lion walked into the room? I probably would! And, yes, a life totally devoid of fear and anxiety would be boring. That's why we love roller coasters and thrill rides. (But we want *safe* rides—we don't want to die riding them.)

So when does legitimate fear become an incapacitating phobia? What are the differences between anxiety, fear, and panic attacks? In order to live a healthy life, every Christian needs answers to these important questions. Let's start by defining terms.

Fear

Fear is the most basic instinct of every living creature. An animal without fear will soon become some predator's lunch. Fear is the natural response when our physical safety and mental well-being are threatened.

Legitimate fears are learned, and they're vital for our survival. For instance, falling off a chair at an early age helps you develop a healthy respect for heights. Animals have even been designed by God to cause us to react in fear for our own protection. A rattlesnake shakes his tail, telling everyone to "watch out" and "back off"—"I'm here, and I'm not happy." You probably don't need to even see the snake to be afraid. All you have to do is hear the sound of that rattle, and you physically respond by jumping away. You don't have time to think, *There's a snake—I should jump away.* You just do it!

Phobias

Phobias are *irrational* fears that compel us to do irresponsible things or hinder us from doing what we should. Phobias reveal problems in our past development, and they can indicate a lack of faith in God.

Fear is different from anxiety and panic attacks because fears and phobias have a legitimate object. In fact, phobias are categorized by their objects:

acrophobia	fear of high places
agoraphobia	fear of open or public spaces
arachnophobia	fear of spiders
claustrophobia	fear of enclosed places
gephyrophobia	fear of crossing or passing under bridges
hematophobia	fear of blood
hydrophobia	fear of water
monophobia	fear of being alone
nyctophobia	fear of the darkness
pathophobia	fear of disease

scholionophobia
   (school phobia). . . . . . . fear of school
toxiphobia. . . . . fear of being poisoned
triskaidekaphobia . . . . . . fear of the number 13
xenophobia . . . . fear of strangers
zoophobia . . . . fear of animals

Real Fear Objects

In order for a fear object to be legitimate it must have two *attributes* (characteristics or qualities): It must be *present* and it must be *powerful*. For instance, those who struggle with claustrophobia don't sense any fear until they are actually in a confined place, like being stuffed upside down in a sleeping bag. Just the thought of such a possibility causes some people to shudder. (By the way, the womb is an enclosed place, so it is safe to assume that a newborn infant doesn't have claustrophobia. Somehow the fear of being confined is learned—as are most fears. So, it can be unlearned.)

Fear is based on how we view things. For instance, one time a United States customs official saw a small, colorful snake near the Arizona border. He fearlessly picked it up and deposited his trophy in a jar. Later he learned that it was a coral snake—which looks harmless but is actually one of the most venomous snakes in the western hemisphere. He went pale with fear when he learned the true danger he'd been in. Even though the fear object wasn't present, the memory of picking it up made him react as though it were.

Most of us have been trained to believe that poisonous snakes are legitimate fear objects. As you read this sentence, you probably sense no fear of snakes because there aren't any in the room with you. What if someone were to throw a rattlesnake into your room and it landed at your feet *(present* and *powerful)*? You would probably be terror-stricken. Now suppose a *dead* snake is thrown at your feet *(present,* but not *powerful).* You wouldn't sense any fear—provided you were sure it was dead. The fear object is no longer legitimate when one of its attributes is removed.

The core of most phobias can be traced to the fear of *death,* of *man,* or of *Satan.* For example, the fear of dying is likely the root of claustrophobia. The Bible clearly teaches that we have no need to fear any of these phobia sources, because in each case God has removed one of their attributes.

For instance, the reality of physical death is always *present,* but the *power of death has been broken.* Paul teaches that the resurrection of Christ has rendered physical death no longer powerful: "Death is swallowed up in victory. 'O death, where is your victory? O death, where is your sting?'" (1 Corinthians 15:54-55). Jesus said, "I am the resurrection and the life; he who believes in Me will live even if he dies, and everyone who lives and believes in Me will never die" (John 11:25-26). In other words, those who have accepted Christ as their Savior will continue to live spiritually even when they die physically. With such a belief, Paul—and every believer—can say, "To me, to live is Christ and to die is gain" (Philippians 1:21). The person who is free from the fear of death is free to live today.

The phobias rooted in the fear of *man,* or people, include rejection, failure, abandonment, and even death. Jesus said, "Do not fear those who kill the body but are unable to kill the soul; but rather fear Him who is able to destroy both soul and body in hell" (Matthew 10:28). As an example, the number-one reason young Christians don't share their faith is the fear of man or, more specifically, the fear of rejection by their friends and looking like a failure.

The Way Fear Should Be

Christ's words in Matthew 10 teach that it is *God* whom we should fear. Two of God's attributes make Him the ultimate fear object in our lives: He is *omnipresent* (always present) and *omnipotent* (all-powerful). To worship God is to ascribe to Him His divine attributes. We do this for our sake—to keep fresh in our minds that our loving heavenly Father is always with us and is more powerful than any enemy.

The fear of God destroys all other fears because God rules supreme over every other fear object—including Satan. Even though "your adversary, the devil, prowls around like a roaring lion, seeking someone to devour" (1 Peter 5:8), he has been defeated (he is still present, but not powerful). Jesus came for the very purpose of destroying the works of the devil (1 John 3:8). "When He had disarmed the rulers and authorities, He made a public display of them, having triumphed over them through Him" (Colossians 2:15).

We have been trained by our culture to be fearful of people and of "things that go bump in the night"—but we have not been trained to fear God. The scary movies of the '50s featured King Kong, Godzilla, and the "Blob," along with the typical parade of psychopathic killers. Then the cultural tide shifted to the occult and alien abductions, or hostile invasions that put the whole human race on the brink of extinction. Soon a new form of horror movie was born, one where there was no hero who won over the bad guy at the end. The bad guy or demon won, and nothing could defeat him! (What a tragic contradiction to what the Bible really says!) Satan loves this because he wants to be feared and worshiped.

We worship persons and objects when we elevate their perceived power and value above God. But only God should have that place in our lives. It's Him we are to worship and fear. The Bible says, "The fear of the LORD is the beginning of wisdom" (Proverbs 9:10).

Anxiety

Anxiety is different from fear in that it lacks an object. People are anxious because they are uncertain about a specific outcome, or they don't know what is going to happen tomorrow.

It is perfectly normal to be concerned about the things we value. That's why we need to distinguish between temporary anxiety and an anxious trait that goes on and on. A state of anxiety exists when we're concerned *before* a specific event. We can be anxious about a college entrance exam to be taken, or our performance at the state track meet, or the threat of an incoming storm. Such concern is normal, and it moves us to take the right action. But we also need to remember that the vast majority of the things we fear and are anxious about never happen or lead to real harm.

Generalized Anxiety Disorder

In a *generalized anxiety disorder,* a person shows an anxious trait over a long period of time. (Over at least a six-month period, obsessive worrying must occur more days than not.) Youth who struggle with this disorder experience continual anxiety and worry. They will worry about at least two stressful life circumstances, such as relationships, health, or ability to perform well in school, and usually they struggle with a large number of worries and spend a lot of time and energy doing it. The intensity and frequency of the worrying is always overdone when compared to the actual problem. In fact, the worrying is usually more harmful than the outcome of the problem they were first concerned about.

Most young people don't like to live in an anxious state and will do almost anything to relieve it. Many alter their minds with drugs, alcohol, food, or music. But Peter reminds us to cast all our anxieties on Christ—the ultimate cure—because He cares for us (1 Peter 5:7).

Panic Attacks

In a *panic attack,* your heart feels like it is beating too fast, or you're light headed—so you begin to let your mind panic. Even though these problems may at first make you feel like something is very wrong, they are typically not life-threatening. Once you receive a proper diagnosis of the condition, you can usually return to a normal life, often without medication.

Panic attacks can occur unexpectedly without any apparent reason. They're labeled "attacks" because the panic is not preceded by any abnormal thinking or the approach of danger. They may or may not occur with any existing phobias. For example, if you fear being attacked and start avoiding public places, your original concern or fear can evolve into agoraphobia (fear of open or public spaces). Between 1 and 2 percent of the American population suffer from just panic attacks, but 5 percent suffer from panic attacks complicated by agoraphobia.

Could some of these cases be spiritual? When we speak at student conferences, we often ask how many young people have been suddenly awakened in the grip of paralyzing fear. Perhaps they feel pressure on their chest or experience the sensation of choking or being choked. When they try to respond physically, they feel like they can't move or speak. At least 30 percent of those attending our conferences have had such an experience.

A secular doctor or counselor would call these symptoms a "panic or anxiety attack." They won't call it a "fear attack" because they can't identify the object of the fear or point to some external cause for the attack. We believe these are spiritual attacks (though not all panic attacks are direct spiritual attacks). Understanding biblical truth can help a person resolve this kind of attack in a matter of seconds.

The Whole Answer

The fear of God overcomes all other fears. Anxiety is overcome by faith in God, and spiritual attacks are overcome by worshiping God in our daily walk. More than 300 biblical passages tell us not to fear, but little relief will come to you in your struggle with phobias if you are just told not to fear. That is not the whole answer. Although Christ is the answer, and the truth will set you free, as a suffering young Christian you need to know *how* to connect with God and *how* the truth sets you free.

We absolutely need God, and we also need each other in order to live a free and productive life. Would you be fearful of a neighborhood bully if you had an armed escort of marines constantly at your side? Would you be anxious for tomorrow if someone with billions of dollars promised to take care of you? How much more confident would you be if you knew that God would never leave you and promised to meet all your needs according to His riches in glory (see Hebrews 13:5; Philippians 4:19)? No human can do this for you, and no amount of money can accomplish what only His presence can.

To get our hands on all this, we need a renewing—a changing of our minds. In order to live and walk by faith, we must know the truth. Jesus is the truth (John 14:6). His Word is truth (John 17:17). The Holy Spirit has come to lead us into all truth (John 16:13). That truth will make us free (John 8:32).

Jesus said, "Peace I leave with you; My peace I give to you; not as the world gives do I give to you. Do not let your heart be troubled, nor let it be fearful" (John 14:27). We have the answer in Christ. As children of God, we don't have just the words of

Christ, we also have the *very presence of His life with us and within us.*

To be sure, things we learned before coming to Christ have to be unlearned through repentance and by the renewing of our minds. We need to change our view of things to God's view and turn our backs on anything that doesn't go God's way.

Nobody can fix our past, but by the grace of God we can be free from it. Only in Christ are we assured victory over our fears. He is the only One we can cast our anxieties upon—the only One in whom we can find the peace of God that passes all understanding.

Only in Christ do we have authority over the god of this world. Jesus, the "Prince of Peace," came to set the captive free. There is no condemnation for those who are in Christ Jesus (Romans 8:1). We can't solve a problem unless we admit we have one—and we all do. The unconditional love and acceptance of God is what allows us to go to Him in total honesty. We *can* cast our anxiety onto Him because He *does* care for us.

By the way, depression is often the unwanted companion or consequence of anxiety disorders. We recommend that you read Neil and Dave's book *Stomping Out Depression*, which explains how to overcome it. Depression is a natural reaction to losses in life or the sense of being helpless and hopeless. But God is our hope, and we can turn to Him for help, as David writes: "Why are you in despair, O my soul? And why are you disturbed within me? Hope in God, for I shall again praise Him, the help of my countenance and my God" (Psalm 43:5).

WE BELIEVE THAT EVERY YOUNG CHRISTIAN can be free from any anxiety disorder and learn to live free in Christ. We believe there is a peace of God that surpasses all understanding that will "guard your hearts and your minds in Christ Jesus" (Philippians 4:7). Jesus said,

> Come to Me, all who are weary and heavy-laden, and I will give you rest. Take My yoke upon you and learn from Me, for I am gentle and humble in heart, and you will find rest for your souls. For My yoke is easy and My burden is light (Matthew 11:28-30).

As you read the words of this book, remember that God is with you right now and will *never* turn away from you. So nothing can stop you from receiving the truths that God has just for you in this book. Read on—our prayer is that the God of all strength and wisdom will guide you each step of the way until every fear is destroyed.

—Neil, Dave, and Rich

A World Living in Fear

No one will ever forget September 11, 2001. Like December 7, 1941, it has been called "a date which will live in infamy." At 8:45 A.M., American Airlines Flight 11—a Boeing 767 carrying 92 passengers—slammed into the north tower of the World Trade Center in New York City. At 9:06 A.M., United Airlines Flight 175—with 65 passengers aboard—was flown into the south tower. In less than an hour, at 10:00 A.M., the south tower collapsed. Twenty-nine minutes later, the north tower, weakened by its imploding twin, came crashing to the ground. The two 110-floor giants were destroyed. World Trade Center Plaza was now Ground Zero.

The terror didn't stop there, however. American Airlines Flight 77, with 64 on board, hit the west side of the Pentagon at 9:40 A.M., and another aircraft—United Airlines Flight 93—crashed in Shanksville, Pennsylvania, headed for Washington, D.C. Back in New York, as the fire continued to burn at Ground Zero, another casualty of the attacks was about to fall. At 5:25 P.M., World Trade Center Building Number 7 finally gave in to the flames and falling debris. Thousands were dead, more than in the 1941 attack on Pearl Harbor.[1]

Terrorism had stabbed at America before and left wounds, but on 9/11 it hit and pierced our heart. Never before had an attack on American soil been so brazen nor had such devastating consequences. On that day innocent victims of terrorism had left home, kissing their wives, husbands, and children goodbye, not knowing they would never return.

The terrorists attacked and destroyed more than just people and buildings that day—they attacked our sense of safety, security, and significance. The terrorists stabbed at our core needs and replaced them with fear. Since the events of 9/11, everyone can relate to fear. Who knows where or when the next terrible attack will occur? We are a world living in fear.

BUT IN STARK CONTRAST TO THAT FEAR, the Bible reminds us that "God has not given us a spirit of fear, but of power and of love and of a sound mind" (2 Timothy 1:7 NKJV). Fear is a thief. It tears down our faith, plunders our hope, steals our freedom, and takes away our joy of living the abundant life in Christ. Phobias are like the coils of a snake—the more we give in to them, the tighter they squeeze. Tired of fighting, we give in to the temptation and surrender to our fears. But what seems like an easy way out becomes, in reality, a prison of unbelief—a fortress of fear that holds us captive.

According to statistics, nearly 20 million Americans (about 1 in 13) suffer from a phobia at some point in their lives. Three to six million suffer from panic disorders, while the same number are afflicted with OCD (obsessive–compulsive disorder). Up to ten million Americans struggle with persistent anxiety (generalized anxiety disorder) every year.[2]

Not included in the above numbers are the more subtle fears that keep young Christians from stepping out in faith and living an abundant life in Christ. Most Christians who struggle with anxieties suffer from ones that wouldn't be classified as disorders, but the anxieties do hinder their personal growth. These believers might have a limited understanding of what it means to be a child of God, and they might lack the assurance of God's presence in their lives.

Causes and Cures—and Our Concerns About Them

What are the root causes of anxiety disorders, and what is the cure, or how are they healed? If a panic attack is simply a physical disorder—and we acknowledge it can be—then medication along with a balanced regimen of nutrition and exercise is the proper prescription. We also acknowledge that medication can be helpful, and in some cases, essential for the treatment of panic disorder and for its assistance in overcoming fear and anxiety. In extreme cases of fear and anxiety, it is very difficult to process biblical truth until the physical symptoms have been reduced through medication.

But we have four concerns about causes and cures. First, we are deeply concerned that too many prescriptions for health and wholeness leave out Jesus and ignore the reality of the spiritual world. To truly help someone, we must take into account *all* reality that affects the whole person—body, soul, and spirit. We thank God for doctors, who have the unique goal of treating the physical body, but we also delight in God's provision for our souls and spirits. We need both the hospital and the church.

Second, we are concerned over where our faith and hope are placed. God and His Word are the only legitimate objects for our faith. God is the One who comforts us as we place our hope in Him (2 Corinthians 1:4,10). The medical model does not treat the whole person or take into account all reality. And no human doctor can be a valid object for our faith.

Third, we are concerned about priorities. Today we seem to seek every possible natural explanation first—and if that doesn't work, then there is nothing left to do but pray. When Jesus talked about the problem of anxiety, He said, "Seek first His kingdom and His righteousness, and all these things will be added to you" (Matthew 6:33). James said, "Is anyone among you suffering? Then he must pray" (James 5:13). The *first* thing a Christian should do about anything is pray, and this is especially true for any mental, emotional, or spiritual problem.

Fourth, we need to avoid the extremes. One extreme is to believe that taking any medication or seeking any medical help is a lack of faith. Our physical bodies must be fed in order to survive, and they will occasionally need medication because we live in a world filled with germs and viruses. The other extreme is to place our hope solely in medication. We have seen both errors in our churches and youth groups. Some people will seek medical help but not personal counsel, while others may seek counsel but won't consult a medical doctor. Unfortunately, many young people who struggle with anxiety don't seek help at all, and therefore they suffer needlessly.

The Ultimate Cause

In one sense, all our problems can ultimately be traced back to the fall of Adam and Eve. God created them to be spiritually and physically alive. They were able to totally relate to God. But when Eve was deceived and Adam sinned, they both died spiritually. They were separated from God. Physical death would also be a side effect, but one that didn't happen immediately. God's perfect creation was thrown into more chaos than a herd of cheerleaders with no pom-poms.

As we saw earlier, fear was the first emotion recorded in Scripture after the fall. Adam said, "I was afraid because I was naked;

so I hid myself" (Genesis 3:10). When the resurrected Christ first appeared to His disciples He found them cowering in fear of the Jews. He simply said to them, "**Peace be with you**" (John 20:19).

Anxiety disorders often reveal a separation—a disconnection—from God and the lack of involvement in a supportive church or youth group. However, simply telling people that they must be born again and find a few Christian friends falls short of the mark, though it is a good beginning. **Rather, we all have to go through a growth process that involves the renewing of our minds. What self-confidence we had before Christ must be replaced by confidence in God.**

The self-righteous and overconfident Paul had to be struck down in order to become an apostle. Only then could he say, "Put no confidence in the flesh" (**Philippians** 3:3).

We need to remember that freedom and wholeness are found only in Christ. A true knowledge of our heavenly Father and a deep understanding of what it means to be a child of God are essential keys to overcoming the shackles of fear and anxiety.

No "Delete" Button

Have you ever wondered why you still feel the same fears and *— Good* struggle with many of the same anxieties you did before you came *Question* to Christ? To answer that we have to understand what did and did *for discussion* not happen at salvation.

Because of the fall, we were all born physically alive but spiritually dead (Ephesians 2:1). We had neither the presence of God in our lives nor the knowledge of His ways. Consequently, we all learned to live our lives independently of God. This learned independence is what the **Bible calls** "the flesh."

The moment we were born again, we became new creatures in Christ. Old things passed away and new things came (2 **Corinthians** 5:17). We received the mind of Christ (1 **Corinthians** 2:16)

suicide question

and the indwelling Holy Spirit, who will lead us into all truth. But we still struggle with many of the same fears and anxieties because being saved does not instantly renew our minds. All those old fleshly thoughts and habits programmed into our "computers" are still there. There is no "delete" button in our memory banks. That is why the Bible says, "Do not be conformed to this world, but be transformed by the renewing of your mind, so that you may prove what the will of God is, that which is good and acceptable and perfect" (Romans 12:2).

Every believer in Christ has a filter through which the Word of God passes in its "journey" from the eye and ear "gates" to the heart. The truth of God's Word is sifted through a grid of previously learned experiences and the emotions associated with them. That grid consists of that person's belief system about the world—including his or her perception of God, self, and others.

Suppose you're being raised by parents who say you'll never amount to anything—and you believe it. Throughout childhood, you kept getting the message "You're a loser!" Your parents would walk up to you each day and form an "L" with their thumb and index finger on their forehead. Now, as a new Christian, you are confronted with an opportunity that would prove your parents wrong if you were successful in it. Plus, you just recently read in the Bible that you can do all things through Christ who strengthens you (Philippians 4:13). But that nagging little voice that was programmed into your mind for years says, "You'll never amount to anything." Your negative identity and fear of failure all but drown out the awesome truth you just read.

When the Sink Is Clogged

Some young people's thoughts are so clogged with the garbage of past abuse, neglect, disappointments, betrayal, and lies that they remain locked in chains of fear, anxiety, and unbelief. They can't seem to connect with the truth of God's Word. In severe cases, simplistic advice like "You just need to trust God" or "God says it, just obey it" is about as helpful as yelling at a clogged sink, "Why don't you just open up?" The drain will stay plugged until you pour down the clog remover. The clog is the young believer's own unbelief or lack of repentance. In reality, they *can* connect with the truth, but they don't *believe* they can. Years of conditioning have taught them not to. Their fears are more real to them than the presence of God and all His promises.

How to break free from the bondage of conditioning? James asks this question: "What is the source of quarrels and conflicts among you?" (James 4:1). He says it is self-centered and worldly living. His answer is, "Submit therefore to God. Resist the devil and he will flee from you. Draw near to God and He will draw near to you" (4:7-8). If you try resisting the devil without first submitting to God, you will have a dogfight. If you submit to God but don't resist the devil, you stay in bondage. The following testimony reveals the necessity to have a whole answer:

> I lived from one surge of adrenaline to the next. My entire life was gripped by paralyzing fears that seemed to come from nowhere and everywhere—fears that made very little sense to me or anyone else. Six years of professional counseling offered little insight and no change in my level of anxiety.
>
> After two hospitalizations, trips to the emergency room, repeated EKGs, a visit to the thoracic surgeon, and a battery of other tests, my panic attacks had only worsened. By the time I came to see you, full-blown panic attacks had become a daily feature.
>
> It has been three weeks since I've experienced a panic attack! I have gone to malls and church services. I've played for an entire worship service, and even made

it through Sunday school with peace in my heart. I had no idea what freedom meant until now. When I came to see you, I had hoped that the Truth would set me free, but now I know it has! Friends have told me that even my voice is different.

When you live in a constant state of anxiety, most of life passes you by because you are physically/emotionally/mentally unable to focus on anything but the fear that's swallowing you. I could barely read a verse of Scripture at one sitting. It was as though someone snatched it away from my mind as soon as it entered. Scripture was such a fog to me. I could only hear the verses that spoke of death and punishment. I had actually become afraid to open my Bible. These past weeks, I have spent hours a day in the Word, and it makes sense. The fog is gone. I am amazed at what I am able to hear, see, understand, and retain.

Before I read your book *The Bondage Breaker,* I could not say "Jesus Christ" without feeling sick. I could refer to "the Lord" with no ill effect, but whenever I said "Jesus Christ" my insides went into orbit. I can now call upon the name of Jesus Christ with peace and confidence...and I do it regularly.

This woman's sink was clogged. She got unclogged when her pastor took her through the "Steps to Freedom in Christ," which helped her resolve her personal and spiritual conflicts. (The "Steps to Freedom" are included in the back of this book.)

The apostle Paul spoke of these spiritual "clogs" or strongholds when he wrote,

> Though we live in the world, we do not wage war as the world does. The weapons we fight with are not the weapons of the world. On the contrary, they have divine

power to demolish strongholds. We demolish arguments and every pretension that sets itself up against the knowledge of God, and we take captive every thought to make it obedient to Christ (2 Corinthians 10:3-5 NIV).

How Strongholds Are Developed

Strongholds are repeated patterns of thinking, feeling, and acting that are deeply ingrained in a person's personality. They are similar in concept to what psychologists call "defense mechanisms," which are unhealthy ways of coping with life. How are they formed? Because we begin our lives without Christ, our minds get programmed from the world around us.

There are two primary ways that such attitudes and beliefs are formed. First, they come from your environment through your experiences, such as the home you were raised in, the schools you attended, the community you played in, and the youth group you attended (or didn't attend). Second, they come from your environment through traumas: a death or divorce in the family, frightening experiences, and severe traumas such as rape and other violence.

Strongholds are habitual patterns of thought that have been burned into our minds over time or by the intensity of traumatic experiences. They are revealed in our personalities, and they greatly influence how we live and respond to life. For instance, if you see an adult who is afraid to ride an elevator, you can be sure he or she has had a negative experience that led to this fear. No one is born with such a fear. Nor is anyone born with an "inferiority complex." Inferiority complexes are *acquired*—from being raised in a performance-based society and being compared to those who appear to be smarter, stronger, or better-looking.

The world system we were raised in is totally different from our new citizenship in the kingdom of God. "He rescued us from the domain of darkness, and transferred us to the kingdom of His beloved Son" (Colossians 1:13). Not only has our citizenship changed, but we personally have changed as well. "You were formerly darkness, but now you are Light in the Lord; walk as children of Light" (Ephesians 5:8). We have to learn how to walk as children of light because we previously learned to live without Christ.

Strongholds of Fear

Anxiety disorders are strongholds, or defense mechanisms, that were acquired in order to survive, cope, or succeed in life. Though everyone is afraid at one time or another, a person with a stronghold of fear might be described as "timid," "fearful," or even "phobic." Though everyone worries once in a while, a person with a stronghold of anxiety might be described as "a worrier," or "insecure," or perhaps even "a control freak." Rather than live by faith in God, they try to cope with their fears and anxieties with their own natural resources.

Strongholds can form at any time in life, but they are most often formed in early childhood. They can set a pattern for life that, apart from the grace of God, will remain until the grave. Here's how fear became a stronghold in one person's life:

> I have lived with crippling, chronic fear for literally all of my life. When I was about seven years old, I had an experience in grade school that kicked it off. I was feeling very sick one day at school, and the teacher would not let me go home. I wanted to go very badly, but I felt trapped and experienced my first panic.
>
> From there on it became a constant circle. The feelings that I felt that day as a young girl were so scary that I spent the rest of my childhood and teenage years

doing everything I could to avoid them. It got so bad that I actually quit school in ninth grade and was tutored at home. Then, at about age 14, I committed myself to a children's home for intense in-house therapy. It was either that or end my life.

It was extremely hard to live there, but it did break the fear cycle because they forced me to push through the fear to attend classes.

But as I returned home, it all gradually came back. I lived in my bedroom, which was my safe place. But eventually I started waking up in the middle of the night with terrible, gut-wrenching panic attacks. It was awful, and my parents had no clue as to what was wrong with me.

I spent years visiting doctors and different specialists to no avail. All my fear and panic stayed inside. I could be in a "number 10" panic—and most everyone around me would not even know. I think I felt such shame because of it. I didn't want anyone to know that I was sick. It put so much stress on my family, and I hated being the problem.

The World Gives Us Reasons to Fear

In the world, we'll always find people and circumstances that can cause us to be fearful. The above story reveals a serious case of phobic avoidance because the girl eventually quit school and started being tutored at home. She had been so frightened and humiliated by her teacher that she established a pattern of doing everything she could to avoid that kind of pain again. It became so severe that she "lived in her bedroom." Although her story doesn't say this, it would not be surprising to find that she became agoraphobic (irrationally fearful of open or public spaces) after the onset of her panic attacks. At any rate, fear was the controlling mechanism in her life, and she suffered badly from a social phobia.

Social phobias, such as in the story above, involve the fear of being watched, embarrassed, humiliated, rejected, or scorned while doing something in front of other people. The most common example of this type of phobia is the fear of public speaking. A similar example is a Christian's fear of sharing his or her testimony or witnessing to an unbeliever. Others include the fear of eating in public, using public restrooms, and meeting new people.

The girl's story illustrates the typical means of coping with social phobias: eliminating threatening circumstances from your life. This obviously poses real problems if you're afraid to go to work or school. For example, school phobia is a big problem for some youth who are unwilling to leave the security of home and parents and take the risk of coping with the school environment, which they perceive as threatening.

How We Relate to the World

Our minds are a clean slate when we're born, but we do have a natural appetite—sin. We were born spiritually dead in our sins with an Adamic nature (see Ephesians 2:1-3). God will forgive "sin; yet He will by no means leave the guilty unpunished, visiting the iniquity of fathers on the children and on the grandchildren to the third and fourth generations" (Exodus 34:7). Though we were born equal in the sight of God, we were not born with equal opportunity. Some parents are better than others at helping their children develop. God has not equally distributed gifts, talents, or intelligence. Also, each person also has a God-given temperament that affects how he or she relates to the world.

This means that some people are more open to anxiety disorders than others. For instance, not every child would have reacted to an insensitive teacher in the way the girl in the story did. Some kids, if they were feeling sick and were forbidden to go home, would have reacted in anger. Others probably would have accepted their fate and withdrawn. Still others would have thrown a temper tantrum. Some of those differences in reactions have to do with our God-given temperaments and personal choice.

Christ Gives Us Freedom and Lasting Change

Now for the good news. Long before we came to know Him, God knew us (see Ephesians 1:4). "Those whom He foreknew, He also predestined to become conformed to the image of His Son" (Romans 8:29). He redeemed us from the futile way of life we inherited from our forefathers (see 1 Peter 1:18). Every one of us was born vulnerable and needy. We need spiritual life, forgiveness, acceptance, security, significance, and an identity that stands the test of time and pain. Paul painted a clear picture of our spiritual condition and God's remedy for it in Romans 5:6-8:

> While we were still helpless, at the right time Christ died for the ungodly. For one will hardly die for a righteous man; though perhaps for the good man someone would dare even to die. *But God demonstrates His own love toward us,* in that while we were yet sinners, Christ died for us (emphasis added).

The girl who struggled with social phobia has an encouraging "part two." It is a testimony of finding freedom and lasting change in Christ.

> I was not raised to know God. I searched for Him when I was 14, when I felt that I could not take it another minute. But I had no one to whom I could go. I tried

praying to Him to help me, but felt that He was so far away. If He created me, I couldn't understand how He could allow me to live in such misery.

From then on I felt anger and bitterness toward Him. I chose not to seek Him.

My crippling fear did not get any better. It changed a lot as I got older, probably because I had to learn how to fake it even better. I hated it when friends would want to camp out for an evening because I still couldn't do it. But I would pretend. I would tell them, "Sure— what time and where?" But then the panic would set in, and I would scramble for excuses to get out of it.

My sister was a Christian and was committed to praying for me. She prayed for 12 long years, never giving up. Praise God! I finally called her in the middle of the night after an evening of misery, feeling again that I could not take living inside this jail anymore. There was a world outside of me that I could never really touch or feel, and it killed me.

I wanted life so badly. And I wanted to be free, so I called her in tears and asked her how to find this Jesus she kept telling me about. She prayed with me on the phone, and I spent the rest of the night reading verses she had given me. They all referred to freedom in one way or another.

Freedom! I felt such hope. That started my journey of renewal. I spent all those years in such crippling fear— fear of fear. It was not knowing that scared me so bad. I learned about what physically happens when we fear something. I continued learning about anxiety and fear and what it can do. Understanding these things was what really set me on the road to peace.

My nerves are pretty shot inside. But my head and my spirit are at peace. I still struggle with going on long vacations. The old tapes still try to run in my head, but I override them with the truth—the truth being that Jesus is with me all the time and I have nothing to fear.

Indeed, I can do all things through Christ who strengthens me. I found that verse when I first became a Christian, and I still rely on it today. Praise God!

Stomping Out Fear

Read:
2 Timothy 1:7

Reflect:

How do we see fear gripping our world?

How have the tragic events of 9/11 affected you personally?

Why do we need to understand the fall of mankind to better understand fear?

How are strongholds of fear developed? Can you identify any strongholds in your life?

What is a social phobia? Can you give some examples? What does our environment do to us that can make us develop phobias?

What is your greatest fear? How is it currently present and powerful in your life? How is God more powerful and more present than your fear(s)?

Respond:

Dear heavenly Father, I admit that at times I let fear control me. I ask You to reveal to me the limited power of my fear.

Lord, why should I fear the unknown when the Bible tells me that You have not given me a spirit of fear, but of power, love, and a sound mind. I choose to put my trust in You, Lord, and turn from my fear. In the sermon on the mount, Jesus talked about the problem of fear and said, "Seek first His kingdom and His righteousness, and all these things will be added to you." Lord, I am turning right now to You and Your ways, and I am seeking Your kingdom. I am asking You, Lord, to give me Your strength so that I might be strong and courageous. In Jesus' name I pray, amen.

(See 2 Timothy 1:7; Matthew 6:33.)

Two Fearful Heart

IT IS HARD TO IMAGINE THAT Adam and Eve ever felt anxious or fearful when they were spiritually alive and lived in the presence of God. Sin, however, disconnected them from their loving heavenly Father, and their fallen descendants have struggled with fear and anxiety ever since. In Psalm 38, a depressed David wrote, "I confess my iniquity; I am full of anxiety because of my sin" (verse 18). David's answer was to confess his sins, place his hope in God, and pray for salvation and help from the Lord (see Psalm 38:15,22).

We don't want to give the impression that every anxiety disorder can be cured by prayer and confession. However, from the beginning we do want to say that salvation, genuine repentance, and faith in God are essential to live a life of freedom in Christ. Salvation brings forgiveness of sins and spiritual–eternal life to the believer. The moment we are born again, the Spirit of God takes up residence in our lives, and we are again connected to God "in Christ." His Spirit speaks to our spirits, telling us that we are children of God (Romans 8:16).

It's easy to forget how much God loves you and that He sacrificed His Son especially for you. Here's a great story to remind you of the Father's love.

After a few hymns, the pastor stood up and introduced a guest speaker. With that, an elderly man stepped up to the pulpit to speak. "Three people boarded a boat: a father, his son and the son's friend. They were sailing off the Pacific Coast," he began. "Then a fast-approaching storm blocked any attempt to get back to shore. The waves were so high that even though the father was an experienced sailor, he could not keep the boat upright, and the three were swept off the boat and into the ocean."

The old man hesitated for a moment, making eye contact with two teenagers who looked somewhat interested in his story. He continued, "Grabbing a rescue line, the father had to make the most excruciating decision of his life. Which boy should he throw the other end of the line to? He only had seconds to make the decision. The father knew that his son was a Christian, and he also knew that his son's friend definitely was not. The agony of his decision could not be matched by the torrent of waves. As the father yelled out, "I love you, son!" he threw the line to his son's friend. By the time he pulled the friend back to the capsized boat, his son had disappeared beyond the raging swells into the black of night. His body was never recovered."

By this time, the two teenagers were sitting straighter in the pew, waiting for the next words to come out of the old man's mouth. "The father," he continued, "knew his son would step into eternity with Jesus. He could not bear the thought of his son's friend stepping into an eternity in hell. Therefore, he sacrificed his own son. How great is the love of God that He should do the same for us."

With that, the old man turned and sat back down in his chair as silence filled the room. After the service ended, the two teenagers were at the old man's side. "That was a nice story," politely started one of the boys, "but I don't think it was very realistic for a father to give up his son's life in hopes that the other boy would become a Christian."

"Well, you've got a point there," the old man replied, glancing down at his worn Bible. A big smile broadened his narrow face, and he once again looked up at the boys and said, "It sure isn't very realistic is it? But I'm standing here today to tell you that story gives me a glimpse of what it must have been like for God to give up His Son for me. You see...I was the son's friend to whom the father tossed the rescue line."[1]

Have you accepted Christ as your personal Savior? If you haven't yet, would you take a few moments and pray to receive Him right now? Consider these important facts:

1. God loves you and wants to have a personal relationship with you (John 3:16).

2. Our sin cuts us off from God so we can't have a personal relationship with Him and experience His love (Romans 3:23).

3. Jesus Christ is the only cure for our sin. Through Him you can know God personally and experience His love (Romans 5:8).

4. We must individually receive Jesus Christ as Savior and Lord—then we can know God personally and experience His love (John 1:12).

You can receive Jesus Christ right now by faith through prayer:

Dear Lord Jesus, I want to know You personally. Thank You for dying on the cross for all my sins and for rising from the dead. I open the door of my life to You right now and receive You as my Savior and Lord. I put my trust in You alone, Jesus, to forgive all my sins and give me eternal life. Thank You that I am now a new person in Christ and Your child. Amen.

Connected to God—But Still Double-Minded

#2

We have found one common factor with the Christian youth that we have counseled, regardless of what their problem was. They didn't know who they were "in Christ," and they didn't understand what it means to be children of God. Where was the inner sense of "Abba, Father" (Galatians 4:6)?

To be spiritually alive means that our inner self is united with God. We have become a temple of God because His Spirit dwells within us (Romans 8:10-11). Spiritual life, our union with God, is most commonly portrayed in the New Testament as being "in Christ." For every verse that says Christ is in us, there are ten verses that say we are "in Christ" or "in Him."

Given that every believer is spiritually alive in Christ and our souls are in union with God, why do we still struggle with anxiety and fear? The answer is twofold. First, in a positive sense a certain amount of fear is needed for our safety and survival, and we *should* be anxious or concerned for those things we care about. Second, as we saw in the last chapter, in a negative sense our minds were programmed to live without God. Everything we learned before we came to Christ is still programmed into our memory banks—and there is no "delete" button. Therefore we must be transformed by the renewing of our minds.

#3 To be anxious in a negative sense is to be *double-minded*. We're conforming to the old pattern of the flesh at the same time we're in Christ. James says that a double-minded person is unstable in all his or her ways (see James 1:8). This is clearly illustrated by Jesus in Matthew 6:24-25: "No one can serve two masters; for either he will hate the one and love the other, or he will be devoted to one and despise the other. You cannot serve God

and wealth. For this reason I say to you, do not be worried about your life." The answer to anxiety, according to Jesus, is to seek first the kingdom of God and trust our heavenly Father to take care of us.

Plan A Versus Plan B

Since we were all born dead in our sins, we learned to live our lives without God's guidance and influence. Let's call this "Plan B": man's way of reason, intuition, and experience (see the diagram below). Before Christ, all we had was plan B.

Plan A is God's way, which we accept by faith. We learn God's way by choosing to study and believe His Word. This is made possible only by the indwelling presence of God, as the apostle Paul indicates: "A natural man does not accept the things of the Spirit of God, for they are foolishness to him; and he cannot understand them....But we have the mind of Christ" (1 Corinthians 2:14-16).

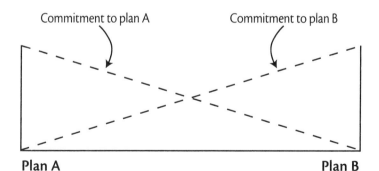

We also have the Holy Spirit, who will lead us into all truth (John 16:13).

God's plan is not just a better way to live—it always includes His vital relationship with His children. Without the life of Christ, we cannot live successfully according to God's plan. We learned in the past how to cope, succeed, and survive without God—and in the process, we developed many fears, phobias, and insecurities. Without eternal life, how could we not fear death? Unless we are secure in Christ, how could we not be anxious for tomorrow? We would have to live in denial or simply not care. Without God we have no choice but to trust in our own pitiful strength and resources.

False Security

Plan B is always lurking in the back of our minds. These flesh patterns, strongholds, and defense mechanisms will always suggest a way to deal with life's problems on a human level. This is evident when the struggling young Christian asks, "Can I totally trust God, or should I just whisper a prayer and then deal with life as though I am solely responsible for making my own way in this world?" (Talk about double-minded!) Can we say that we trust God if we defend ourselves, meet our own needs, and make our own living using our own resources? When we choose plan B we are cutting ourselves off from the intimacy and love that only Christ can give us.

Here's a description of that kind of love in a story about a father, a son, a tragedy, and a great victory.

> The 1988 Armenian earthquake needed only four minutes to flatten the nation and kill thirty thousand people. Moments after the deadly tremor ceased, a father raced to an elementary school to save his son. When he arrived, he saw that the building had been leveled. Looking at the

mass of stones and rubble, he remembered a promise he had made to his child: "No matter what happens, I'll always be there for you." Driven by his own promise he found the area closest to his son's room and began to pull back the rocks. Other parents arrived and began sobbing for their children. "It's too late," they told the man. "You know they are dead. You can't help." Even a police officer encouraged him to give up.

But the father refused for eight hours, then sixteen, then thirty-two—for thirty-six hours he dug. His hands were raw and his energy gone, but he refused to quit. Finally, after thirty-eight wrenching hours he pulled back a boulder and heard his son's voice. He called his boy's name: "Arman! Arman!" and a voice answered him, "Dad—it's me!" The boy added these priceless words: "I told the other kids not to worry. I told them if you were alive, you'd save me, and when you saved me, they'd be saved, too. Because you promised me, 'No matter what, I'll always be there for you.' "[2]

What would you do if you were trapped in a crumbled fallen building? What would go through your mind? The circumstances of life and our past experiences want us to embrace fear. Can I really give all my fears to Jesus? It's so easy to fall back on old ways of coping with life when the pressure is on.

But for the Christian who is alive in Christ, what power is greater than God—and what situation is impossible for Him? We have a heavenly Father who will dig through the rubble of our lives until we are free from every bondage and fear. We can even be like Arman and tell all those around us that God is going to save us if we just trust in Him. Insecurity is depending on temporal things that we have no ability to control. Security is depending on eternal life and values that no one and no thing can take away from us.

What About Your Physical Side?

Fear and anxiety are the emotional reactions—the felt reactions—to our understanding of life events. They don't occur in a vacuum. Anxiety disorders are a life problem, and to solve them we must consider how our whole person is responding to threatening events or potential disasters.

In the original creation, God formed Adam from the dust of the earth and breathed life into him. This union of divine breath and earthly dust is the makeup of every born-again child of God on earth. We are both physically and spiritually alive. We have an outer person and an inner person, a material part and an immaterial part.

The material or physical part relates to the external world through our five senses. We can taste, smell, hear, feel, and see. The inner person relates to God through the soul and spirit. Unlike the creatures of the animal kingdom, which operate out of instinct, we have the capacity to think, feel, and choose. Since we are "fearfully and wonderfully made," it makes sense that God would create the outer person to go along with the inner person.

Here's an example of how thinking, feeling, and choosing work. Again, we'll use a snake story. Suppose you were taking a walk through the Arizona desert and came upon one of those scaly creatures. Your eyes see it and send a signal to the brain. Your emotional response is completely dependent upon how your mind was previously programmed. If you have no prior knowledge of snakes, your emotional response would be more one of curiosity than fear.

Now suppose you have some prior knowledge of snakes, but not enough to make a distinction between those that are poisonous and those that aren't. Your emotional response would likely be instant fear if you mistakenly believe that all snakes are legitimate fear objects. However, if your prior knowledge of snakes is quite extensive and it's easy to immediately see that the snake is not poisonous, your response would again be more one of curiosity than fear. A little knowledge can make something appear dangerous, but a lot of knowledge sets you free.

Two people can look at the same situation and respond totally differently because they don't have the same experience or belief system or both. That is why you hear people say to one another "I don't know what you have to worry about" or "What are you afraid of?" To those who are knowledgeable, it doesn't make any sense that others are so afraid or anxious. That is why the truth sets us free.

Truth and Reality

If what we perceive or choose to believe does not reflect truth, then how we feel does not reflect reality. Let's see how this applies to anxiety. Suppose you work at McDonald's and you have a very intimidating boss. Word is circulating around the restaurant that he wants to see you, which makes you very anxious. You don't know why he wants to see you, so your mind begins to entertain several possibilities. *Maybe he wants to fire me or chew me out for that simple little mistake I made last week. I think I'll quit and rob him of the satisfaction of lording it over me!* The more you entertain such thoughts, the more anxious you become. Finally the hour of your appointment with him arrives, and you are a bundle of nerves. Gingerly you enter his office—only to be greeted by all the top brass, who are there to congratulate you for the promotion you are about to receive. Had you known the truth before the appointment, your emotional state would have been totally different.

The same holds true for fear. When I was in high school, I delivered the morning paper. One day I couldn't because of a back injury I had sustained in a wrestling tournament. So I drove the car while my mother carried the papers to the door. I forgot to tell her about this certain vicious watchdog that came growling and snarling around the corner whenever anyone approached his house. Talk about fear! When that dog came around the corner, my poor mother just about had a heart attack. I had also forgotten to tell her about the chain that would stop the dog from getting near her. There was no fear of that dog in my mind because I knew the truth. My mother, however, didn't have my prior knowledge and experience.

When You Overload on Stress

Let's apply this same logic to the problem of stress. When external pressures put demands on our physical system, our adrenal glands respond by secreting hormones into our body. In other words, our bodies automatically respond to external pressures. This is the natural "fight or flight" response to the pressures of life. If the pressures persist too long, our adrenal glands can't keep up, and stress becomes *distress*. The result can be physical illness—or we may become irritated with things that wouldn't bother us physically or emotionally in less stressful times.

Why then do two people respond differently to the same stressful situation? Why do some actually seize the opportunity and thrive under the pressure, while others fall apart? What is the difference? Although we may differ considerably in our physical condition, the major difference lies in our mind—that is, in what we believe. It isn't just the external factors that determine the degree of stress. We all face the pressures of deadlines, schedules, trauma, and temptations. The major difference is how we mentally interpret the world around us and process that information in our brains.

Our mind can choose to respond by trusting God for the assurance of victory (plan A) or to be the helpless victim of circumstances (plan B). For instance, the Israelites saw the giant Goliath in reference to themselves and were paralyzed by fear. David saw the same giant in reference to God, and he said, "Let no man's heart fail on account of him; your servant will go and fight with this Philistine.…The LORD who delivered me from the paw of the lion and from the paw of the bear, He will deliver me from the hand of this Philistine" (1 Samuel 17:32,37). Faith in God (what we believe) greatly affects how we interpret and respond to fear objects and impending danger.

David exercised faith, and therefore, he had a lot of confidence in God. He also had a whole heart for Him. Righteous people who walk with God see reality—the complete picture—through the eyes of faith in ways that others don't. For instance, the servant of the prophet Elisha saw an army with horses and chariots surrounding the city where they were staying and cried out,

> "Alas, my master! What shall we do?" So [Elisha] answered, "Do not fear, for those who are with us are more than those who are with them." Then Elisha prayed and said, "O LORD, I pray, open his eyes that he may see." And the LORD opened the servant's eyes and he saw; and behold, the mountain was full of horses and chariots of fire all around Elisha (2 Kings 6:15-17).

On the other hand, the unrighteous see things that aren't there: "The wicked flee when no one is pursuing, but the righteous are bold as a lion" (Proverbs 28:1).

Fear is an adrenaline rush. When our minds perceive the presence of a fear object, a signal is sent from our brains to our nervous systems. Our muscles become rigid and tense as the alarm races through our bodies. But it is critically important to understand that the adrenal glands do not initiate the release of adrenaline. They are *responders,* not initiators. The hormone is released into the bloodstream *after* the brain has recorded the external inputs and the mind has interpreted the data. And the brain can only function according to how it has been programmed.

The Presence of God Affects Our Bodies

Salvation brings the presence of God into our lives, but there is no immediate physical change in our bodies. Similarly, what physical changes can you observe in your computer when you slip in a new program? But even though the same number of hardware components exist in the machine, the screen reveals the presence of the new program. The electronic flow through the computer has changed. Likewise, we should begin to live differently if a new "program"—Jesus—is loaded into our lives; our eyes have been opened to the truth, and we have been given the power of the Holy Spirit, enabling us to live by faith.

There is growing evidence that the programming of our minds—that is, how we choose to think—affects our brain chemistry. We certainly know that our physical body is affected the moment we think anxious thoughts or perceive a fear object.

The presence of God in our lives will slowly affect our total being, including the physical aspects. According to the words of Paul, "He who raised Christ Jesus from the dead will also give life to your mortal bodies through His Spirit who dwells in you" (Romans 8:11). This is evident when we walk by the Spirit since "the fruit of the Spirit is love [the character of God], joy [the opposite of depression], peace [the opposite of anxiety], patience [the opposite of anger], kindness, goodness, faithfulness, gentleness, self-control; against such things there is no law" (Galatians 5:22-23). The connection between the initiating cause (the Spirit of truth working in our lives) and the end result (self-control) is the mind, which directs the brain, which in turn regulates our glands and muscular movements.

Biblical Faith Leads to Wholeness

Jesus asked the blind men, " 'Do you believe that I am able to do this?' They said to Him, 'Yes, Lord.' Then He touched their eyes, saying, 'It shall be done to you according to your faith' " (Matthew 9:28-29). The external power of Jesus was made effective by their choice to believe. In other words, the Lord chose to bring about a physical healing through the channel of belief. Is this not true in every other aspect of life? We are saved by faith (Ephesians 2:8), sanctified—set apart to be like Christ—by faith (Galatians 3:3-5), and we walk, or live, by faith (2 Corinthians 5:7).

God never bypasses our minds; we are transformed by the renewing of our minds. He makes possible the renewing of our minds by His very presence in our lives. We respond in faith by choosing to believe the truth and living by the power of the Holy Spirit, not carrying out the desires of the flesh (Galatians 5:16). Jesus is "the way [how we ought to live], and the truth [what we ought to believe], and the life [our spiritual union with God]" (John 14:6). Even the operation of spiritual gifts incorporates the use of our minds. Paul put it all together by saying, "I will pray with the spirit and I will pray with the mind also; I will sing with the spirit and I will sing with the mind also" (1 Corinthians 14:15).

What About Medication?

Scripture instructs us to live in peace and warns us not to be anxious or fearful. In other words, the focus of Scripture is primarily on the software (the mind), not the hardware (the brain). Can we have a hardware problem? Of course! Organic brain syndrome, Down's syndrome, and Alzheimer's disease are all hardware problems, and there is little that can be done to help them. The best software in the world won't work if you pull the plug on your computer or damage it beyond repair. So the brain must be chemically in balance with a normal production and flow of neurotransmitters in order for the mind to function.

Should a Christian take prescribed drugs for emotional problems? Suppose you are suffering from acid indigestion. Should you take medication to relieve the heartburn? Most people would, and there is nothing wrong with getting temporary relief—but it is not a long-term answer. Your body is saying, "Stop feeding me this junk!" You probably need to consider changing your eating habits. And there is also the possibility that you have a more serious stomach illness, such as an ulcer or cancer.

Garbage In, Garbage Out

Computer programmers use the term *GIGO*, which means "garbage in, garbage out." If we put garbage into our minds, we will live a polluted life. Jesus said, "The good man out of the good treasure of his heart brings forth what is good; and the evil man out of the evil treasure brings forth what is evil; for his mouth speaks from that which fills his heart" (Luke 6:45). Paul says we have to take every thought captive to the obedience of Christ (2 Corinthians 10:5). It doesn't make any difference whether our thoughts originate from the television set, the Internet, the radio, a book, a speaker, from our own memory banks, from the pit, or from our own unique thinking. We take *every* thought captive to the obedience of Christ.

If what you're thinking is not true according to God's Word, then don't pay attention to it. Instead, do what the apostle Paul says to do: "Brethren, whatever is true, whatever is honorable, whatever is right, whatever is pure, whatever is lovely, whatever is of good repute, if there is any excellence and if anything worthy of praise, dwell on these things" (Philippians 4:8). You don't get rid of negative thoughts by trying not to think of them. You overcome them by choosing the truth—and keep choosing it until the negative thoughts are drowned out or are completely replaced by the truth. If you want to experience the freedom that Christ purchased for you and the peace of mind that passes all understanding, then choose to think only those thoughts that line up with the Word of God.

> In the country church of a small village, an altar boy serving the priest at Sunday mass accidentally dropped the cruet of wine. The village priest struck the altar boy sharply on the cheek and in a gruff voice shouted, "Leave the altar and don't come back!" That boy became Tito, the communist leader.
>
> In a cathedral of a large city, an altar boy serving the bishop at Sunday mass accidentally dropped the cruet of wine. With a warm twinkle in his eye the bishop gently whispered, "Someday you will be a priest." That boy grew up to become the Archbishop Fulton Sheen, one of the greatest Christian Catholic communicators of the twentieth century.[3]

It is probably fair to say we have all been in both boys' shoes at one time or another. The question is, what will we choose to believe about ourselves? If we put garbage into our minds and dwell on all the negative things that have ever been said about us, then we will become negative, ugly people. But if we take *every* thought captive to the obedience of Christ, we will walk in the freedom that Christ promised us. We must reject what the world says about us and accept that what Christ says about us is really true—whether we feel like it's true or not.

Virus Scan

If you own a computer, you have no doubt been warned about all the viruses out there that can cause a serious meltdown in your system. Computer viruses are often not accidental—they are intentional. For instance, they may come from store-wrapped software that gets contaminated by a disgruntled employee. Perhaps he's mad at the company he works for and wants to damage their image. And some devious people have purposefully created programs designed to introduce a destructive virus into any system that accesses them. That's why most computer systems have programs that scan for viruses. And so should we!

It is not always easy to detect a virus in our own belief system because the major strategy of the enemy is deception. Every Christian is subject to tempting, accusing, and deceiving thoughts. The most devious of Satan's schemes is deception—because if you were tempted you would know it, if you were accused you would know it, but if you were deceived you wouldn't know it. That's why we are to put on the armor of God. We're to stand against Satan's fiery darts aimed at our minds by taking up the shield of faith.

The father of lies has been at work from the very beginning, even at creation. Eve was deceived, and she believed a lie. Paul writes, "I am afraid that, as the serpent deceived Eve by his craftiness, your minds will be led astray from the simplicity and purity of devotion to Christ" (2 Corinthians 11:3). That is why Jesus prays for those who want to follow Him, "I do not ask You to take them out of the world, but to keep them from the evil one....Sanctify them in the truth; Your word is truth" (John 17:15,17). Commenting about the latter days of the church age, Paul wrote, "The Spirit explicitly says that in later times some will fall away from the faith, paying attention to deceitful spirits and doctrines of demons" (1 Timothy 4:1).

We have seen evidence of this all over the world. Young people struggle with their thoughts, have difficulty concentrating, and some actually hear "voices." These "voices," or negative thoughts, are usually self-condemning, suicidal, delusional, and phobic—and they result in feelings of guilt, shame, fear, and anxiety. How could students and youth not feel fearful and anxious if they were thinking those kinds of thoughts?

A secular therapist or doctor would likely see the cause of these feelings as a chemical imbalance and prescribe an antipsychotic or tranquilizer to treat the anxiety disorder. We don't want to rule out that possibility altogether, but serious questions need to be asked. How can a chemical produce a personality or a thought? How can our neurotransmitters randomly fire in such a way as to produce a thought that we are opposed to thinking? We believe that these negative thoughts are patterns of the flesh learned from living in a fallen world—or else they are the "flaming arrows" from Satan that Scripture clearly warns us about. A therapist with a secular worldview would not even consider such possibilities.

Diagnosis: A Battle for Your Mind

In our experience, the symptoms we've described above often reveal a battle for the mind. Instead of suggesting new or additional medication, we help young people resolve their personal and spiritual conflicts by submitting to God and resisting the devil (James 4:7). You cannot experience the fruit of the Spirit if you are believing a lie, dabbling in the occult, holding on to bitterness, boasting pridefully, living in rebellion, or sinning. Those issues must be resolved so that you can experience the peace of God.

The minds of young persons who are struggling with anxiety disorders are riddled with mixed-up thinking and lies—about themselves, God, and their circumstances in life. Connecting with God through genuine repentance and renewing our minds to this truth of His Word will result in every born-again Christian experiencing this truth: "The peace of God, which surpasses all comprehension, shall guard your hearts and your minds in Christ Jesus" (Philippians 4:7).

Stomping Out Fear

Read:
2 Corinthians 10:5

Reflect:
What is the one thing that most struggling people have in common?

In this chapter we talked about "plan A" and "plan B." What is plan A, and what is plan B? What plan are you currently following in your life?

What does the term *GIGO,* or "garbage in, garbage out" mean in our lives? How do Christians run a virus scan in their spiritual life?

What is the most devious of Satan's schemes that we talked about in this chapter?

Why is it so important that we put on the whole armor of God? What happens to us if we don't?

Respond:

Dear heavenly Father, I want to take every thought captive in obedience to Christ. I admit that I have at times filled my mind with the garbage of this world. I have allowed the world, my flesh, and the devil to determine what I think and believe. I choose now to let the Holy Spirit scan my mind to see if I am believing any lies about God or who I am in Christ. I don't want to live in fear and anxiety. I want to destroy every fear with the understanding that God is greater than all my fears and anxieties. So I tell Satan and all of his evil workers to leave my presence. I choose to give my mind and body to the Lord Jesus Christ, and I choose to believe His truth. In Jesus' name I pray, amen.

Overcoming the Fear of Man

Three

THE FEAR OF GOD IS THE ONE FEAR that destroys all unhealthy fears. "The fear of man brings a snare, but he who trusts in the LORD will be exalted" (Proverbs 29:25). We are living in bondage if we fear man more than God.

What is actually holding us in bondage, though, is our own lack of knowledge and belief in God. The fear of man is a stronghold that must be broken in order for us to experience the freedom to live as Jesus did. In the following testimony, notice how a stronghold of fear was developed.

> When I was 11, my family moved to an upscale town in New York that was predominantly white. The folks there weren't used to living next to blacks. I remember standing at a water fountain in the sixth grade and having a classmate ask me if I had a tail. I remember walking past a school bus and having a boy hold up a drawing of a man with a noose around his neck and scream that it was me.
>
> I recall being so starved for acceptance that I thought it was a compliment when someone told me, "We don't consider you to be a nigger. You're different."

> Against this backdrop was a dysfunctional home where my mother filled my head with lies. She told me I was gay because I didn't date. She said I was stupid because my grades stunk. She guaranteed that I would die by the time I turned 16 because my life was so futile.
>
> This hostility shaped my view of myself. By the time I was 18, I was so stripped of confidence that I couldn't look a person in the eye. I was filled with doubt and fear, and I struggled with a poor self-image.

A deep-seated insecurity and fear of man can form in our lives when negative labels are slapped onto our souls at a young age. Like scarlet letters, these labels broadcast our faults (or someone's perception of our faults) to the world around us. A sense of personal shame and inferiority breaks our spirit.

In the testimony above, it is obvious how a young man such as this would fear rejection from people. He experienced the sting of racial slurs. His mother, instead of affirming him, called him gay and stupid and told him his life was futile and he was doomed to die young. Like a puppy brutally whipped, he learned at an early age that it is easier to steer clear of people and not make waves than it is to risk being ridiculed and rejected.

When I hit puberty, I thought I had contracted a terminal illness. Almost overnight my body declared civil war against me. My face broke out, my teeth stuck out (so I had to endure the private prison of braces), and my height and weight went in one year from five feet, six inches and 120 pounds to six feet and 120 pounds! I wasn't skinny—I was *skeletal*. I became a convenient target for other insecure kids at school, who were glad to find someone in worse shape than they were!

At first I tried to fight back against the sneers and rude comments of my peers, but after a while I gave up. Feeling ganged-up on by the world, I withdrew in fear and shame. Tired of walking out of the lunch line and finding no one to eat with in the cafeteria, I chose to bring my lunch to school and eat in a vacant classroom by myself. It was a very sad and lonely time of life. I retreated into my own little world. I felt increasingly angry against "the establishment" that had created such an unfair system of acceptance and rejection based on physical appearance.

My fear of rejection by people drove me deeper and deeper into myself. Without Christ, there was only darkness inside. My room became my only safe place—and it might have become my tomb if not for Jesus. My story, and the one preceding it, are examples of how the fear of man can put a stranglehold on the life of a person without Christ. But children of God also struggle under the effects of this stronghold as well, especially when we confuse our expectations—and what others expect of us—with what God expects from us.

Only One Legitimate Fear Object

We become subject to the fear of man when we are not secure in the unconditional love and acceptance of God. Also, it's easy to forget that God is omnipresent (everywhere) and omnipotent (all-powerful) when confronted by various fear objects we can see—because God is invisible. That is why we need to worship Him. When we ascribe to Him His divine attributes in worship, we are keeping our minds filled with the knowledge of His presence.

God drove this point home when He corrected His people through the prophet Isaiah for their faintheartedness in the face of human enemies:

> I, even I, am He who comforts you. Who are you that you are afraid of man who dies and of the son of man who is made like grass, that you have forgotten the LORD

your Maker, who stretched out the heavens and laid the
foundations of the earth, that you fear continually all day
long because of the fury of the oppressor, as he makes
ready to destroy? But where is the fury of the oppressor?
(Isaiah 51:12-13).

In these verses, God presents the huge difference between
man and Himself. The bottom line is that people live and die like
grass, but God is the Creator of heaven and earth (including the
grass!). Why be afraid of man, who can only harm you for a limited time, when God is the eternal, all-powerful comforter? A
legitimate fear object has to be both present and powerful, as we
saw in "The Fear Factor." As long as we live on planet earth,
people will be present. But what power do they have over us that
cannot be overcome in Christ? None! We may be rejected by
people, but we will always be "choice and precious in the sight of
God" (1 Peter 2:4).

Feel the Fear, but Trust in God

Fear of man and faith in God cannot be operative at the same
time. We will always struggle with tempting thoughts and fearful
feelings, but they do not have to keep us from making the choice
with our will to walk by faith in God. That is courage—making
the choice to walk by faith and do what's right even in the face of
fear. Being alive and free in Christ doesn't mean that we will
never feel fear. It means that such fears no longer have any power
over us if we exercise our faith in God.

There will be times when you will be afraid or hesitant to
speak the truth in love, and the fear of man will motivate you to
lie to others. Giving in to those fears will only compound the
bondage. Paul tells us to

lay aside the old self, which is being corrupted in accor-
dance with the lusts of deceit, and…be renewed in the

> spirit of your mind, and put on the new self, which in
> the likeness of God has been created in righteousness
> and holiness of the truth. Therefore, laying aside false-
> hood, speak truth each one of you with his neighbor, for
> we are members of one another (**Ephesians 4:22-25**).

If you are afraid to say no when God has said no, you are a servant of man. The apostle Paul said of himself, "Am I now trying
to win the approval of men, or of God? Or am I trying to please
men? If I were still trying to please men, I would not be a servant
of Christ" (**Galatians 1:10** NIV). You cannot serve two masters.
Trying to keep from ruffling the feathers of those around you will
eventually cause you to compromise your stand for Christ.

The Courage to Share

Paul preached the gospel of grace knowing that it ran cross-
current to the preaching of the Jewish religious leaders who
wanted to bring new Gentile converts under the yoke of the law.
Paul ferociously attacked their false teaching and took some
painful shots while protecting the church from heresy. How many
believers are scared into silence when they ought to be pro-
claiming from the rooftops what God has done for them in
Christ? How many times do we sense the inner urging of the Spirit
of God to witness for Christ, but we keep quiet with the excuse
that we don't want to appear pushy, preachy, or insensitive?

Do we value our own safety and security more than the soul
of another person? Most of us would emphatically say no, but
when an opportunity arises to share our faith we are paralyzed
by fear. Where does that fear come from? "God has not given us
a spirit of fear, but of power and of love and of a sound mind"
(**2 Timothy 1:7** NKJV).

Phobias drain our power and make physically strong people
feel weak and paralyzed. They take away love for others and drive

us into a whirlpool of self-centeredness. Fear of mankind is mutually exclusive of the love of mankind. Love is self-giving, but fear is self-protecting. Love moves us toward others—fear causes us to shrink from others. Fear steals our wisdom and clear thinking and replaces it with confusion and error.

Dr. Bill Bright's personal life and ministry as founder and president of Campus Crusade for Christ is a testimony of the power of the Holy Spirit in witnessing. In his bestselling book *Witnessing Without Fear,* he wrote,

> Witnessing for our Lord is something we all know we should do....Yet witnessing is an activity we frequently shrink from. To intrude in someone else's life seems not only threatening but blatantly presumptuous. We fear offending the other person, fear being rejected, fear doing an inadequate job of representing our Lord and even being branded a "fanatic."[1]

In the chapter "Why More Christians Don't Witness," Dr. Bright suggests three main reasons for believers' timidity in evangelism: spiritual lethargy (not being filled with the Spirit because of sin), lack of proper training, and listening to the devil's lies.[2]

It stands to reason that if the gospel is the power of God for salvation, then the enemy will do all he can to keep God's people from being the ambassadors He has called them to be. Satan is the father of lies, and if we believe him we will keep silent. The truth will set us free, but lies will keep us in bondage.

Here are some of the specific lying "lines" the enemy tries to feed us, according to Dr. Bright:

- Mind your own business—you don't have any right to force your views on someone else.
- You're going to offend this person. Don't say anything.
- That person will think you're a fanatic.

- This person will say no, and you'll be embarrassed.[3]

Notice that each one of the devil's lies is targeted at our own insecurities. We naturally want other people to like and respect us. We feel more comfortable when things are peaceful—free of conflict or controversy. And so far too often we keep quiet…or we talk about everything under the sun except Jesus and our faith in Him.

Cassie's Story

April 20, 1999, started like any other day. Cassie Bernall slipped on her beloved velvet Doc Martens, grabbed her backpack, and headed out the door through the backyard, over the fence, across the soccer field to high school, which was only a hundred yards away. Little did Cassie know that she was about to enter a battle zone. In a short time, the whole campus would be cordoned off and surrounded by an army of police and SWAT teams.

Just before 11:00 A.M. an explosion ripped through Columbine High School, and shots began to fill the normally serene atmosphere.

Cassie was in the library studying *Macbeth* for an English class. She had only been there for a short time when a teacher bolted in, yelling that there were kids with guns in the hall. One of the teachers yelled for everyone to get under the tables, but no one was listening. It didn't seem to make sense. As the shots down the hall grew closer, one of the teachers found a phone and called 9-1-1.

Two boys, one named Eric and the other, Dylan, came into the library. Their voices sounded scary and evil. At the same time, they seemed happy—like they were playing a game and getting a kick out it. They were knocking over tables and chairs, then more shooting started. One of the guys came up to Cassie. They asked her one simple question. "Do you believe in God?" She paused only for a moment, then uttered with singular clarity, "Yes!" They put the gun to her head and pulled the trigger.

When the grisly events of that spring day were finally over, Cassie Bernall's body was found lying under a table close to that of another young girl.[4] The blast that ended her life had taken her away, instantly transporting her from this life to the next. What kind of mastery of her emotions did Cassie have? What kind of bravery captivated her mind, allowing her to state so clearly her fatal identification with her God?

If you were faced with Cassie's question—the ultimate question—would you identify with Christ? Would you overcome your fear to proclaim your faith? I believe you would, because greater is He who is in you than He who is in the world. To sacrifice your life for the cause of Christ, to be a martyr, is almost the greatest sacrifice you as a Christian can make. But there is one sacrifice that is greater. That is to live each and every day for the cause of Christ—and proclaim with boldness God's means of salvation through Christ alone.

What Do We Have to Gain?

As long as we perceive that somebody or something has the power to destroy anything we value, we will be in bondage to that fear object. And that fear will paralyze us into a life of compromise or withdrawal. The coward always asks, "What do I stand to lose?" The courageous person—like Cassie Bernall—always asks, "What do I stand to gain?" One sees the risks, the other sees the opportunities.

Look at David in 1 Samuel 17. King Saul and his soldiers were drawn up for battle against the Philistines in the valley of Elah. Each side was stationed on a mountain with the valley in between.

The Philistine warrior, Goliath, all nine feet, nine inches of him, issued a challenge to the Israelites. He would fight a Hebrew soldier one-on-one, and whoever killed his opponent would bring victory for the whole army. And the losing side would serve the winners. Goliath issued his blasphemous challenge to the Israelite army for 40 days. Here is how God's people responded: "When all the men of Israel saw the man, they fled from him and were greatly afraid" (verse 24).

The young shepherd boy David, however, had enough courage to take on the challenge. Armed only with his slingshot and five smooth stones, he prepared for battle. Saul offered his own armor to David, believing the boy needed man's help to win God's battle.

David knew better. In his young life he had already killed a lion and a bear. The giant would be no more trouble than they were because he knew God was his rescuer. "David said, 'The LORD who delivered me from the paw of the lion and from the paw of the bear, He will deliver me from the hand of this Philistine'" (verse 37). So David confidently went out to meet Goliath and prevailed over him with a sling and a stone, cutting off the giant's head with his own giant sword.

Why was David willing and able to take on Goliath when no one else was? King Saul and his men saw themselves in relation to the giant and trembled. David saw Goliath in relation to God and triumphed. There was no question in the young shepherd's mind that God would deliver this Philistine warrior into his hands.

Could David have been killed? Of course. But that did not seem to even be an issue for him. He knew that his life was ultimately in God's hands, not Goliath's. He valued his relationship with God more than his own life, and in David's eyes, God's glory was at stake. For him, life was nothing compared to the glory of God, and so there was no other alternative than to fight for the honor and name of his King.

A Higher Calling

The apostle Paul said, "To me, to live is Christ and to die is gain" (Philippians 1:21). Put anything else in the formula, and it doesn't work. "To me, to live is my X-box—to die would be total loss." "To me, to live is my snowboard—to die would be total loss." Being free from the fear of death is not a license to commit suicide—it is a means to live responsibly today.

Someone once said, "There is only one life—it will soon be past. Only what has been done for Christ will last." Your God will bring you through anything that life can throw at you. You can face life with boldness and courage even when you're put under some spiritually challenging times. The following true story shows fear is really a challenge to God and His strength, and it shows how God will always provide the courage we need to face each day.

Stand Firm and Trust

Seven young evangelists sailed to the island village of Mei-hwa. The group was led by Watchman Nee, later one of China's greatest Christian leaders. Despite great effort, they were ignored by the villagers. Finally the youngest, Kuo-ching Lee, shouted to a crowd in frustration, "What's wrong with you? Why don't you believe?"

"Oh, we do believe," came back a reply. "We believe in our god, Ta-wang. He never fails us."

Kuo-ching learned that the village staged a great festival for their god every year. For the last 286 years it had not rained on that festival day. And the celebration was only two days away, on January 11. Impulsively, he announced, "I promise you, our God, who is the true God, will make it rain on the eleventh." The crowd took up his challenge.

When Watchman Nee heard about it, he was very troubled and went away to pray. The phrase from 2 Kings 2:14 came to his mind: "Where is the LORD God of Elijah?" He remembered the contest between Elijah and the prophets of Baal on Mount Carmel (1 Kings 18). Convinced that God was going to do a miracle, Watchman told his friends to tell everyone that the Lord God of Elijah would send rain on January 11, a day on which it hadn't rained in almost three centuries.

On the morning of that day, the sun rose in a cloudless sky. The villagers were assured that Ta-wang was the true god after all. Terribly distressed, Watchman began to pray: "Lord, this doesn't look like the rain that You—" Suddenly his prayer was interrupted by the phrase, *"Where is the LORD God of Elijah?"*

As Watchman rose and joined the others over breakfast, he simply prayed, "Father, please accept our prayer as a gentle reminder that You promised to answer the challenge of the demon-god today. Even though not a cloud appears in the sky, we trust in Your promise."

Before he could say "amen," they heard a few drops hit the tiled roof. The villagers hurried to protect their idol, hoisting him onto a platform to be carried down the streets, and as the false priests tried to carry their statue away, it crashed to the ground, breaking its arm and head.

When the storm finally stopped, the head priest quickly fixed the idol and announced that he'd made a terrible mistake. The annual celebration was to have fallen on January 14, not on January 11.

"Lord," Watchman prayed, "give us good weather till then. We have a lot to do." Over the next three days the men evangelized night and day, and 30 villagers confessed Christ.

When the "correct" day came, at the very same hour as before, another huge monsoon hit Mei-hwa. From that moment, paganism's hold on the island was broken. A church was started. And the faith of the seven young men was dramatically strengthened for their upcoming years in God's work.[5]

It would have been easy for the other six evangelists to become fearful and simply leave the island after they had heard about the rash challenge that Kuo-ching Lee had made to the pagan leaders. But instead they prayed and asked God, "What's your will? What's your plan?" Fear often gives us an opportunity to prove that God is faithful and loving. Be careful not to put Him to the test—but when fear rears its ugly head, we have every right to stand firm and put our trust in God, who has overcome all our fears.

Stomping Out Fear

Read:

Romans 8:31-39

Reflect:

We encourage you to do some prayerful soul-searching. Ask the Lord to show you any fears that you have of man, and why. Pray that He would reveal the nature of the hold people have over you. In what way(s) are you finding it hard to entrust yourself to God, who judges righteously?

The *first* thing we do about anything is go to God in prayer. Tell Him openly and honestly who you are afraid of. He already knows, but you need to be in agreement with Him. Ask Him for wisdom to discern why you are afraid.

Second, make sure you are right with your heavenly Father. Have you resolved all your personal and spiritual conflicts? Are you more afraid of the voice of man than you are of the voice of God? What fear objects have you elevated above the fear of God? It is not a sin to feel afraid, but if the fear of man is controlling you, then God is not.

Third, worship God for who He is. Ascribe to Him His divine attributes of omnipotence ("all-powerfulness") and omnipresence ("everywhereness"). Acknowledge the truth of His Word. Thank Him for His unconditional love and acceptance and for His promise of provision and protection.

Fourth, make an honest assessment of what harm people can do to you. This is where your life is tested. Either God is able to make up for what others have taken away, or He isn't. If you believe He is more than able to meet your needs, you can walk by faith even in the face of man's cruelty. If you doubt that He can or will, then fear will rule.

Fifth, remember that none of your pain or suffering has gone unnoticed by your Father in heaven. He knows your needs and hears your prayers.

Finally, stand firm in your faith, knowing that God is for you. You are His child. He will not allow you to be tested beyond what you are able to bear, but will always provide the way of escape so that you may be able to endure (see 1 Corinthians 10:13). Entrust yourself into His hands, for He truly judges righteously. Nothing can separate you from the love of God.

Respond:

Let Psalm 56:1-9 provide the framework for your prayer for freedom from the fear of man:

> *Be gracious to me, O God, for man has trampled upon me; fighting all day long he oppresses me. My foes have trampled upon me all day long, for they are many who fight proudly against me. When I am afraid, I will put my trust in You. In God, whose word I praise, in God I have put my trust; I shall not be afraid. What can mere man do to me? All day long they distort my words; all their thoughts are against me for evil. They attack, they lurk, they watch my steps, as they have waited to take my life. Because of wickedness, cast them forth, in anger put down the peoples, O God!*
>
> *You have taken account of my wanderings; put my tears in Your bottle. Are they not in Your book? Then my enemies will turn back in the day when I call; this I know, that God is for me.*

Overcoming the Fear of Death

Four

IN A 1997 ARTICLE IN *USA Weekend* magazine, a scientific poll of more than a thousand people revealed what Americans fear. The results are fascinating, in that most of the fears are related to the fear of death:

- 54% feared being in a car crash
- 53% feared having cancer
- 36% feared food poisoning from meat
- 35% feared getting Alzheimer's
- 34% feared pesticides from food
- 33% feared being a victim of individual violence
- 30% feared exposure to foreign viruses
- 28% feared getting AIDS
- 25% feared natural disasters
- 24% feared unsafe buildings
- 22% feared being in a plane crash
- 21% feared suffering a work-related injury
- 18% feared being a victim of mass violence [1]

Of course, surveys like these partly reflect current events. "Being a victim of mass violence," for example, would have been much higher on the list if the survey had been taken after the events of 9/11. "Natural disasters" would have been higher in areas recently struck by tornadoes, earthquakes, or floods.

People are afraid of dying. Nine out of ten Americans believe the world is less safe than when they were growing up. Forty percent feel unsafe taking a walk alone at night within a half mile of home. Seven out of ten have taken some precaution to ensure their safety within the past year, such as locking their cars while inside them, locking windows at home, avoiding certain foods, or avoiding chatting with people on the Internet. [2]

Young people are living in great fear of death. For example, almost half the adults between ages 18 to 24 think they have been stalked by a stranger in the past year, a much higher percentage than older adults.[3] In 1997, 49 percent of teenagers were worried about dying, as opposed to just 38 percent in 1988.[4]

A nationwide random telephone survey of more than a thousand preteens made a few years ago showed that 51 percent of them were "very" or "somewhat" concerned about their own death, and 65 percent were worried about their parents' deaths.[5] Another poll showed that 42 percent of 11- to 17-year-olds are worried that they may die young as a result of violence. [6]

Why Are We So Afraid?

These fears are not totally unfounded. Surveys show that 1 in 20 high-school students have at some time carried a gun to school because they fear being attacked.[7] And the statistics don't reveal how many students who carry weapons are in such a mental and emotional state that they might make such an attack. Recent school shootings—and plots (that have been uncovered) to target other students or teachers—have only accentuated fears.

There is no question that TV has burdened each new generation in America with an increasingly unbearable load of fearful images: violent crime scenes (and violent crimes in progress!), airplane-crash footage, teary-eyed disaster victims picking through wreckage, and so on. Like prophets of doom, newscasters would not be caught dead without their share of wailing sirens and flashing police lights. And this doesn't even include what we see on prime-time TV shows and daytime talk shows!

The media must own up to some responsibility for fostering a national environment of fear. But they are only responding to the viewers, who want to see and hear the bad news. People watch car racing with the anticipation of seeing a wreck. Sporting analysts capture all the disasters of the day along with a few highlights in their five-minute segments on the nightly news. They wouldn't show it if people didn't watch. We can't help but develop a greater sense of fear if that is what we continue to subject ourselves to.

Bondage to the Fear of Death

> Since the children share in flesh and blood, [Christ] likewise also partook of the same, that through death He might render powerless him who had the power of death, that is, the devil, and might free those who through fear of death were subject to slavery all their lives (Hebrews 2:14-15).

What is true today in the twenty-first century was also true in the first century—and has been, every century since the fall of man. People are in bondage to the fear of death unless they have eternal life in Christ Jesus, who holds the keys of death and Hades (Revelation 1:18). The following story illustrates how the fear of death can shackle a believer in Christ, and how the truth and power of Christ delivers us from that fear:

When I was five my mother and father took me to a witch doctor to help cure my nosebleeds. My parents were to say a few prayers and then place a silver coin on my forehead. Shortly after the nosebleeds ended, I became obsessed with dying. A tremendous fear came over me that would not subside.

I accepted the Lord. Two years ago the fear of dying came back full-force after I had given my testimony at a Bible-study sharing day. The fear was oppressive.

Every day I chose clothes to wear that I thought would be my death clothes. How was I going to die? The thoughts in my mind were petrifying.

Where were these thoughts coming from? I asked God to remove this fear....I became familiar with all the "fear" Bible verses. It was so overwhelming...I thought I was going crazy.

I came across *The Bondage Breaker*...I was in bondage. I remember crying out to God to show me what was holding me back. I prayed the prayers...and when I came to the part of renouncing my sexual sins I tried to envision every guy I had ever had sex with...what they looked like or what their name was... I prayed for these men...I prayed that their names were written in the Lamb's book of life...I felt the fear leaving me...the fear of being unworthy to stand before God...the fear of getting AIDS...the fear of dying.

This may sound funny, but with every prayer I almost felt a "poof" coming out of my mind. Then I slowly asked the Lord why this fear had plagued me for so long...and I remembered long ago going to the witch doctor...who, to this day, my mom claims was a man of God.

> I truly believe that a curse was placed on my life when I was five. I lived so many years infested with fear. I didn't care how I lived and became a loose girl because I was sure I would never live to see the consequences.
>
> Thanks be to God, from whom all blessings flow, that there truly is freedom in Christ.

There are many origins for the fear of death. The girl in the testimony above was vulnerable due to the aftereffects of an occult "healing" in childhood. The enemy had gained a foothold in her life through the witch doctor's activity. The devil often operates that way. When you turn to him for help, you may get temporary relief in one area but worse bondage in another. The demonic presence was obviously made worse by the girl's public witness for Christ, and the devil sought to shut it down by making her afraid.

Other people struggle with the fear of death because of close calls with death. John, a missionary bush pilot in Africa, had two close calls while flying his plane. He became agoraphobic. By the end of his first term on the mission field, he was barely able to leave the house for any reason. The seeds of fear were planted early in life, as his testimony reveals.

> After so many years of deception that held me in bondage and fear, I am set free in Christ. Praise His name.
>
> At age 14, my hobby was amateur radio. I enjoyed tuning across the bands and finding faraway stations. When lights-out time came, I would turn the amateur radio off, get in bed, plug in an earphone into my AM radio, and continue listening for faraway broadcast stations.

In time I located a station in New York state. At 10 P.M. I heard their news, station ID, and the introduction to the next program, the *CBS Radio Mystery Theater*. From that night on for the next four years I was hooked to that program, falling asleep with images of suspense and fear flooding my mind. If only I had known what I was setting myself up for.

Sometime thereafter a voice began to tell me just when the phone would ring and who was on the other end, without fail.

I was also able to tell my parents secret habits about people that I knew to be true, even when meeting an individual for the first time. Sometime in the future, often years later, my folks would remark on this to each other and ask me, "How did you know?"

After I received my driver's license, the same voice would tell me where the speed traps were on the interstate. My mom once told me during my years at Bible school that I was blessed with tremendous spiritual insight because of all the things I knew and could do. "Spiritual insight" was right; however, it was the wrong kind.

Not always did the voice tell me truth. The voice would actually become rough and tell me to burn my arms with my soldering iron or poke out my eye with a screwdriver. When I would climb my radio tower to repair antennas at 100 feet high, the voice would often tell me to jump off.

The battle for my mind at those moments on the tower was so intense that just trying to keep safety and good practice in the front of my mind would cause great debilitating fear.

> This same fear began motivating my daily activities. Although the voice in my head would often tell me that I was stupid, ugly, dumb, fat, and would never amount to anything, 90 percent of the time it told the truth. So I just kept listening to it.

John found his freedom in Christ when he finally realized that the "voice" was not God at all (as he had sometimes thought), but was the voice of the enemy. The devil, who once held the power of death, is obsessed with death and dying. And he delights in overwhelming people, even God's people, with the fear of death. Satan tormented John until he renounced two spirit guides. One was passed down from his grandmother, and the other had gained entrance during his addiction to scary radio stories.

I had the opportunity to see John six months after he went through the Steps to Freedom in Christ, and he was a changed man. Controlling fear was ancient history for him. When he went back to Africa to collect his possessions (for his transition back to America), he told me he had more ministry in the lives of people in those two weeks than he'd had in the three years before his furlough! People were so amazed by the changes in his life that he would stay up till two or three o'clock in the morning sharing what God had done for him!

FEAR OF DEATH: THE FOUR MAIN ISSUES

The fear of death seems to center on four main issues. We will take a look at each of these areas of fear and see what the Bible has to say about them:

1. The fear of dying and going to hell. (People who fear they have committed the unpardonable sin also fall into this category.)

2. The fear of dying and leaving loved ones behind.

3. The fear of loved ones dying.

4. The fear and horror of the actual dying process (for example, the fear of being brutally murdered, or experiencing terrible pain).

From the outset, it's important to keep in mind that some fears have no basis in the reality of the physical world. Fear always has an object, but in these cases the object is imaginary. The fear originates in the mind, which is the basic characteristic of neurosis. Extremely fearful people see and hear things that nobody else does. Typically that would be called mental illness, which is defined as being "out of touch with reality" and "unusually anxious." However, anybody caught in a spiritual battle for his or her mind would have neither of these characteristics—and there would be nothing physically wrong with that person. We'll explore this possibility further in a later chapter.

Salvation Conquers Death

All those who have never turned from their sins and received the Lord Jesus Christ as Savior by faith *should* be afraid of death! We were all born dead in our trespasses and sins (Ephesians 2:1). Salvation is a free gift of God's grace, but like any gift, it must be received (John 1:12; Romans 5:17). God's forgiveness is received by faith, not by good actions (Ephesians 2:8-9). No amount of spiritual devotion or pious practices will earn us a place in heaven. We cannot save ourselves.

Jesus paid the penalty for our sins when He died on the cross. His resurrection made possible our new spiritual and eternal life in Him. Our responsibility is to humbly admit our helpless state as sinners in need of a rescuing Savior, and trust in Jesus to forgive our sins and give us life.

The moment we receive the Lord Jesus as our Savior, we become children of God. We are chosen and adopted into His family. We become new creations in Christ. The old has passed away, and new things have come! All this He does to the praise of the glory of His grace.

Therefore, we dare not neglect this great salvation. The Word of God brings good news—but also a stern warning: "He who believes in the Son has eternal life; but he who does not obey the Son will not see life, but the wrath of God abides on him" (John 3:36). There is a heaven to be gained and a hell to be shunned. Have you made the decision to trust only in Jesus Christ as your Lord and Savior?

It is not enough to believe in who Jesus was or is. Nor is it enough to feel a sentimental attraction to Him or go to church or youth group. The Bible is clear: You must make a definite decision to receive Him into your life and trust only in Him for your salvation. If you have never made that decision, we urge you to do so right now. Today is the day of salvation (see Hebrews 3:15; 2 Corinthians 6:2).

"Whoever will call upon the name of the Lord will be saved" (Romans 10:13). "As many as received Him, to them He gave the right to become children of God, even to those who believe in His name" (John 1:12). We encourage you to return to pages 41–42 of this book and review the section on receiving Christ.

If you were sincere when you made your decision to trust in Christ, you can also be assured of your salvation:

> These things I have written to you who believe in the name of the Son of God, so that you may know that you have eternal life. This is the confidence which we have before Him, that, if we ask anything according to His will, He hears us (1 John 5:13-14).

There is simply no other way to escape the fear of dying and going to hell than through Jesus. He physically died and was temporarily separated from God so that we would never have to be. And now He is seated at the right hand of our heavenly Father, and He has prepared a place for us in eternity. One day He will come back for us (John 14:1-3).

The moment you chose to receive Christ, He took up residence in your life. Salvation is "Christ in you, the hope of glory" (Colossians 1:27). His Spirit will speak to your spirit, telling you that you are a child of God (Romans 8:16). Spiritual life means that your soul is in union with God. You are "in Christ," and Christ is in you. Here are two more encouraging Scripture passages that proclaim the believer's victory over death and hell!

> O death, where is your victory? O death, where is your sting? The sting of death is sin, and the power of sin is the law; but thanks be to God, who gives us the victory through our Lord Jesus Christ (1 Corinthians 15:55-57).

> Jesus said to her, "I am the resurrection and the life; he who believes in Me will live [spiritually] even if he dies [physically], and everyone who lives and believes in Me will never die" (John 11:25-26).

Unless Christ comes back first, all of us will die physically. But in Christ, none of us will die spiritually. Eternal life is not something you get when you die. In fact, if you don't have spiritual life before you physically die, you will face nothing but hell. But those of us who are in Christ will be separated from our physical bodies when we die and be instantly in the presence of God. Paul says, "We walk by faith, not by sight—we are of good courage, I say, and prefer rather to be absent from the body and to be at home with the Lord" (2 Corinthians 5:7-8).

Remember our formula for conquering fear? To eliminate something as a fear object, only one of its attributes must be eliminated. Physical death is still *present,* "inasmuch as it is appointed for men to die once and after this comes judgment"

(Hebrews 9:27). But God has overcome the *power* of death. "In Christ," it is no longer powerful.

The Unpardonable Sin

Many believers struggle with the fear that they have committed an unforgivable sin. Youth who are tormented by this fear usually suffer in silence. They think they have committed the unpardonable sin by blaspheming the Holy Spirit. Usually this fear is born out of ignorance, or else it is an attack of the enemy. Let's take a look at Mark 3:22-30:

> The scribes who came down from Jerusalem were saying, "He is possessed by Beelzebul," and "He casts out the demons by the ruler of the demons." And [Jesus] called them to Himself and began speaking to them in parables, "How can Satan cast out Satan?…If a house is divided against itself, that house will not be able to stand. And if Satan has risen up against himself and is divided, he cannot stand.…Truly I say to you, all sins shall be forgiven the sons of men, and whatever blasphemies they utter; but whoever blasphemes against the Holy Spirit never has forgiveness, but is guilty of an eternal sin"—because they were saying, "He has an unclean spirit."

It is the unique work of the Holy Spirit to draw people to Christ. Those who come to Christ are the children of God, and their sins and blasphemies are forgiven because they are in Christ. That is why no Christian can commit the unpardonable sin.

If you reject what God's Spirit says about Christ, then you never come to him in the first place. Just think of it! Standing in front of the scribes and Pharisees was the Messiah—Jesus, the Son of God—and they attributed His ministry of delivering people from demonic bondage to the devil. They even accused Jesus of being possessed by Satan! They totally rejected the witness of the Spirit.

We have talked with many young believers who question their salvation and are under heavy conviction. The very fact that they are feeling convicted for their sins is the best evidence that they are Christians, or that the Holy Spirit is convicting them of their sinful nature and leading them to salvation. This is further evidence that they have not committed the unpardonable sin. If the Holy Spirit was not at work in them, their sins wouldn't even be bothering them.

The devil is an accuser. He is like a prosecuting attorney seeking to discredit and discourage a witness on the stand. He points his slimy finger and says, "Aha! You've done it now! There's no hope for you. You've blasphemed the Holy Spirit!" Perhaps you have questioned some spiritual gift, anointed preacher, or apparent supernatural manifestation. Is that blaspheming the Holy Spirit? Of course not. In fact, it could be necessary discernment. Listen to John's instruction: "Beloved, do not believe every spirit, but test the spirits to see whether they are from God, because many false prophets have gone out into the world" (1 John 4:1). A Christian can grieve the Holy Spirit and even quench the Holy Spirit, but that sin is not unpardonable (see Ephesians 4:30; 1 Thessalonians 5:19).

The Bible says "there is now no condemnation for those who are in Christ Jesus" (Romans 8:1). There is a heaven-and-hell difference between the Holy Spirit's conviction and the devil's accusations. If you come under the conviction of the Holy Spirit and turn away from your sin, the matter is over with. But if the devil accuses you and you believe his lies, it never ends—no matter how many times you confess or try to turn away. Satan accuses believers day and night (Revelation 12:10). Such accusing and condemning thoughts are not from the Lord.

To resolve this, *first* you need to know the truth. *Second,* if those accusing thoughts continue, it may be due to some unresolved personal or spiritual conflicts. (In that case, go through the Steps to Freedom in Christ at the end of his book.) *Third,* you must learn to take every thought captive to the obedience of Christ (2 Corinthians 10:5).

Leaving Loved Ones Behind

Our own lives are like "a vapor that appears for a little while and then vanishes away." This means we must adequately prepare for the possibility that our deaths may come before the deaths of those we love.

Ultimately, freedom from this fear comes from realizing that all things, even our loved ones, belong to God. Life is a gift, and He requires us to be good stewards of what He has given to us (1 Corinthians 3:23–4:2). That should motivate us to be responsible, but it shouldn't create a paranoia about things we cannot control. Our heavenly Father knows our needs, and He watches over those He loves.

Jesus clearly warned His disciples that He was not going to be physically on earth for long (Matthew 16:21)—and neither are we. We need to develop an eternal perspective on life, not a temporal one. The psalmist said, "Precious in the sight of the LORD is the death of His godly ones" (Psalm 116:15). That verse doesn't make sense from a temporal perspective, but it makes all the sense in the world from an eternal perspective. Those who have physically died in Christ are with Him, and they are far better off than when they were here.

The apostle Paul preferred to be with the Lord, but he decided to be a good steward of the time allotted to him until God called him home. His example encourages us to do the same:

> To me, to live is Christ and to die is gain. But if I am to live on in the flesh, this will mean fruitful labor for me; and I do not know which to choose. But I am hard-pressed from both directions, having the desire to depart and be with Christ, for that is very much better; yet to remain on in the flesh is more necessary for your sake. Convinced of this, I know that I will remain and continue with you all for your progress and joy in the faith (Philippians 1:21-25).

The Fear of Loved Ones Dying

Life is a gift, a responsibility in which God has given us a measure of oversight, but not ultimate control. If we choose to follow Christ and accept Him as our Lord and Savior, He watches over us. It is He who appoints the time of our birth and the time of our death.

It was a bottom-line faith that moved Job to say, after the death of his children and the loss of his health, "Naked I came from my mother's womb, and naked I shall return there. The LORD gave and the LORD has taken away. Blessed be the name of the LORD" (Job 1:21). Scripture commended Job for his faith, declaring that Job "did not sin nor did he blame God" (verse 22).

The fear of losing a loved one can easily cause us to cross the line from being responsible and protective of loved ones to being overprotective and irresponsible.

This kind of "protection" can masquerade as genuine love, but in reality it is motivated by fear. Because we cannot bear the thought of how much it would hurt us to see our loved ones harmed or killed, we do everything we can to control people and circumstances to avoid experiencing that pain. In the process, we end up creating a stronghold of fear in ourselves and those around us.

We should always help our loved ones exercise godly wisdom and caution in the face of real danger, but we can't always be with them. There's only One who can be with them every moment of the day. Give each of your loved ones over to the Lord for His protection. Use the following prayer, based on Psalm 139, as a guide:

> *Dear Lord, You have searched and known (<u>names of loved ones</u>). You know when they sit down and stand up. You understand all the things that are going on in their minds. You know where they are going and how they will get there. There is nothing hidden from You at all. You even know what they say before they say it.*
>
> *Lord, You put an invisible shield behind them and in front of them and lay Your hand gently upon their heads. This is so wonderful to me and is far beyond my ability to understand. But I thank You for Your protection.*
>
> *I thank You that there is no place they can go where You are not already there. No matter how far they go to the north, south, east, or west, You will lead them. And if they are in danger, You can take hold of them and rescue them at any time. Even in the middle of the night, when I am most afraid of where they might be and what they might be doing, You see what is going on as if it were the middle of the day. Thank You, Lord, that You watch over them while they sleep, warding off unseen dangers that would attack them when they are most vulnerable.*
>
> *You created them, Lord, so You know what they need far better than I do. So I commit them into Your care as their Creator and Father.*
>
> *Take a good look inside me, O Lord, and see what is in my heart. Show me if I am in any way being controlled by fear and anxiety. I know that those things will result in harmful behavior toward my loved ones. Take me by the*

hand, dear Lord, and lead me in Your everlasting way of life.
In Jesus' name I pray, amen.

Fear of the Dying Process

It is one thing to overcome the fear of death, it is another thing to overcome the fear of dying. We can all look forward to seeing our Lord face to face. It is our hope. But nobody looks forward to the process of dying, especially if it is long and painful. Such prospects can cause us to develop a lot of phobias toward diseases, medications, medical tests, and even doctors. Some people don't want to know the truth about their physical condition because they're afraid they can't handle it. Many people try to manage their fears by living in denial. And then there's the possibility of violent death, such as being a victim of a crime.

In her book *Panic Buster*, Bonnie Crandall lists 28 things that she was afraid of, including "weather, passing out, driving, clouds, food, bees, dogs, heights, crossing the street, strong wind, someone in the house, the dark, bathtub water, being alone, gas fumes, buses and taxis, tornadoes and blizzards."[8] She was also afraid to be in places where she might lose control and be embarrassed.

Her comments about this aspect of the fear of death show how irrational fear can be, as well as the power of God to change a life:

> That [being afraid of those 28 things] was long ago. As I look over my list now much of it seems ridiculous. But it certainly wasn't at the time. Also, I must confess, I'd still be afraid if a tornado actually came and I was in or near one. But, at that time I was afraid we'd have a tornado even if it got only a little stormy outside. There didn't even have to be a watch or warning posted!

> I was afraid of the bathtub water because I was
> weak and shaky so much of the time. I felt as though
> I'd pass out and slip under the water and drown. Actu-
> ally, most of these worries do boil down to the fear of
> death, and the good news is that God conquered death
> when Jesus rose from the grave.[9]

Anyone who struggles with the fear of death is caught in the "what if" syndrome. They tend to imagine the worst, even though over 99 percent of the time the worst doesn't happen or isn't even a threat. They are afraid to drive across bridges because they are thinking, *What if the bridge collapses?* They are afraid to eat at a restaurant because they are thinking, *What if I get food poisoning?* There is usually no logical basis for their fear, so it is very hard to reason them out of their mindset. Telling someone who has a fear of flying that an airplane is the safest way to travel will probably not eliminate the fear.

People who are afraid of dying in a violent or painful way often suffer from *hypochondria*. Hypochondria is the overanxious preoccupation with one's health, often resulting in an irrational fear of being seriously or terminally ill. Such people often read medical journals to learn about various illnesses and their symptoms. A normal person may be annoyed by a headache and take an aspirin, but to the hypochondriac a headache is far more ominous. They start thinking, *Maybe I have a brain tumor.* Almost any symptom, no matter how small, can launch a hypochondriac into an emotional spiral of fear. Their primary battle is in their minds.

Even though there are diseases and germs in this world, our focus must be on the healthy balance of nutrition, exercise, and diet. Supplementing our diets with minerals and vitamins, strengthening our bodies with exercise, and getting enough rest will strengthen our immune systems. We should be health-oriented, not illness-oriented.

It's true that the fear of dying painfully or violently has some basis in reality. There really are dangers out there, and some of us will die painfully slow, or sudden and tragic deaths. But those who are obsessed with these fears seem to lack the assurance of God's presence and His sustaining grace. Plus, they have allowed their minds to ruminate on every negative possibility. Instead, they must think about "whatever is true, whatever is honorable, whatever is right, whatever is pure, whatever is lovely, whatever is of good repute"(Philippians 4:8).

Stomping Out Fear

Read:

Psalm 91

Reflect:

Turn to Psalm 91. List out all the things that the passage says you will be rescued or delivered from.

How is the Lord described in the passage? In what ways is His strength described?

Why is the fear of committing the unpardonable sin something we really don't need to worry about if we have accepted Christ as our Lord and personal Savior?

What are the four main issues that center around the fear of death? Of these, which one is your greatest concern or fear? In what way is God more present and powerful than this fear?

People who struggle with the fear of death are caught in what syndrome described in this chapter?

Respond:

Dear heavenly Father, Your Word says that we "do not have a high priest who cannot sympathize with our weaknesses, but One who has been tempted in all things as we are, yet without sin. Therefore let us draw near with confidence to the throne of grace, so that we may receive mercy and find grace to help in time of need." Lord, I draw near to You now and give You my fears. (State each fear out loud.)

I know that You love me and have delivered me from my fears because You are greater than all my fears put together. I choose to put my confidence in You. In Jesus' name I pray, amen.

(See Hebrews 4:15-16.)

Overcoming the Fear of Failure

Five

SADLY, SOME OF OUR FAVORITE HEROES struggle with the fear of failure. You wouldn't think that baseball's leading pitcher in the 2002 season would struggle with fear. But according to a *USA Today* article, Curt Schilling, who earns $10 million a season, pays close to $25,000 a year for a customized program to critique his pitching. "The fear of failure is so great with me," says Schilling. " I want to avoid that miserable four days after a loss by doing anything I can do."[1]

Schilling, who won the 2001 World Series, still grapples with the fear of failure. What's enough success to finally destroy that fear? The question is inappropriate—as if stopping one activity and starting another would help you overcome any fear. It is not our activity that overcomes fear, but rather the truth we choose to believe.

Ask yourself this question. Who is the more successful student, the one who gets a perfect report card—or the one who needs a tutor after school and works three extra hours each day? You can't answer that question, because no two people have the same opportunity or potential.

God has not equally distributed gifts, talents, or intelligence among His children. Suppose two people were created exactly the same. One was born in Connecticut to wealthy parents. The other was born in a remote jungle to parents who couldn't read or write—they had never even seen modern civilization. Both children have a certain potential in life, but how would you define success for either one? They certainly don't have the same opportunities or desires to accomplish the same educational or material objectives.

Paul said, "We are not bold to class or compare ourselves with some of those who commend themselves; but when they measure themselves by themselves, and compare themselves with themselves, they are without understanding" (2 Corinthians 10:12). You lack understanding if you determine your success or failure by comparing yourself with others.

There must be some other standard of evaluation for success by which we can motivate our lives. The first instruction in the Bible on success is given in Joshua 1:7-8 just before the Israelites were about to go into the promised land:

> Be strong and very courageous; be careful to do according to all the law which Moses My servant commanded you; do not turn from it to the right or to the left, so that you may have success wherever you go. This book of the law shall not depart from your mouth, but you shall meditate on it day and night, so that you may be careful to do according to all that is written in it; for then you will make your way prosperous, and then you will have success.

The First Principle of Success

The Israelites' success did not depend on favorable circumstances in the promised land, nor on the cooperation of the Philistines.

They would be successful and prosperous if they understood God's Word and faithfully lived it. To be successful in life, first you have to know God and His ways. That is the first biblical principle of success.

> Thus says the LORD, "Let not a wise man boast of his wisdom, and let not the mighty man boast of his might, let not a rich man boast of his riches; but let him who boasts boast of this, that he understands and knows Me, that I am the LORD who exercises lovingkindness, justice and righteousness on earth; for I delight in these things," declares the LORD (Jeremiah 9:23-24; see also 1 Corinthians 1:31).

Nobody set the standard for success higher than the apostle Paul. He had intelligence, social status, favorable circumstances, and drive. He was the ultimate achiever and leading candidate for theologian of the year when Christ struck him down. Listen to how he describes his "before" and "after" drive for success:

> If anyone else has a mind to put confidence in the flesh, I far more: circumcised the eighth day, of the nation of Israel, of the tribe of Benjamin, a Hebrew of Hebrews; as to the Law, a Pharisee; as to zeal, a persecutor of the church; as to the righteousness which is in the Law, found blameless.
>
> But whatever things were gain to me, those things I have counted as loss for the sake of Christ. More than that, I count all things to be loss in view of the surpassing value of knowing Christ Jesus my Lord, for whom I have suffered the loss of all things, and count them but rubbish so that I may gain Christ (Philippians 3:4-8).

The feeling of success that comes from winning the race, or graduating at the top of the class is very fleeting. What happens when you get there? Does it satisfy? Do you need to climb one rung higher? "What does it profit a man to gain the whole world, and forfeit his soul? For what shall a man give in exchange for his soul?" (Mark 8:36-37). What does satisfy? Take your highest standard of success in terms of appearance, performance, status, and possessions and then ask yourself, "If I were able to accomplish or possess it, would I be forever satisfied?"

There is only one thing that completely and continuously satisfies. Jesus said, "Blessed are those who hunger and thirst for righteousness, for they shall be satisfied" (Matthew 5:6). Nothing else can satisfy like living a righteous life and being intimately related to our heavenly Father. Loving relationships satisfy, but the satisfaction that comes from titles, degrees, possessions, and accomplishments is fleeting at best.

The Second Principle of Success

It took three years in the desert for Paul to move his ladder over to the right wall. He couldn't stay on the top rung and just push it over to the right wall. He had to start on the bottom rung as we all do. But with a new focus he set out in the right direction, and with a determination to succeed, he proceeded to climb:

> Not that I have already obtained it or have already become perfect, but I press on so that I may lay hold of that for which also I was laid hold of by Christ Jesus. Brethren, I do not regard myself as having laid hold of it yet; but one thing I do: forgetting what lies behind and reaching forward to what lies ahead, I press on toward the goal for the prize of the upward call of God in Christ Jesus (Philippians 3:12-14).

Paul was again motivated to succeed, but with a new goal. He pressed on to lay hold of whatever Christ wanted for him. Christ had chosen Paul for a purpose, as He has chosen all of us. To be successful we have to become the people God created us to be. This is the second principle of success. It is also God's will for our lives. The fact that nobody and nothing can keep us from being the person God has created us to be is the good news. Only we can keep that from happening.

We may not have enough time to accomplish what we want in life, but we have precisely enough time to do God's will. We may not be able to reach the position we hoped for, but what position is higher than being seated with Christ in the heavenlies? We can try to make a name for ourselves in the world, but what name could we make for ourselves that is better than being called a child of God?

The Bible doesn't provide any instruction on career choices. I don't think God cares whether you become an engineer, carpenter, or plumber, though He will provide guidance for such career choices. Career choices are dependent upon our God-given capabilities and reasonable opportunities, and God does care what kind of engineer, carpenter, and plumber you are.

It is part of our calling to serve in certain roles, but the roles do not determine who we are. It isn't what you do that determines who you are, it is who you are that determines what you do. So who are you? "Beloved, now we are children of God, and it has not appeared as yet what we will be. We know that when He appears, we will be like Him, because we will see Him just as He is. And everyone who has this hope fixed on Him purifies himself, just as He is pure" (1 John 3:2-3).

The difficulties and trials of this world can add to our fear of failure if we have the wrong definition of success. But they actually contribute to the right goal of proven character, and that is where our hope lies. Difficulties and trials cannot destroy us, but they do reveal who we are, and they help us become who God created us to be. There is no crisis we can't come through as better people if that is our definition of success.

The Third Principle of Success

Peter wrote, "As obedient children, do not be conformed to the former lusts which were yours in your ignorance, but like the Holy One who called you, be holy yourselves also in all your behavior; because it is written, 'You shall be Holy, for I am Holy'"(1 Peter 1:14-16). Who we are is far more important than what we do, because what we do flows from who we are. The scriptural order is character before career and maturity before ministry. Eventually this should lead to accomplishing something, "for we are His workmanship, created in Christ Jesus for good works, which God prepared beforehand so that we would walk in them" (Ephesians 2:10).

We can't just sit around. Jesus said, "Let your light shine before men in such a way that they may see your good works, and glorify your Father who is in heaven"(Matthew 5:16). We have all been given certain gifts by God that He expects us to use to His glory. Paul wrote, "Let a man regard us in this manner, as servants of Christ and stewards of the mysteries of God. In this case, moreover, it is required of stewards that one be found trustworthy" (1 Corinthians 4:1-2).

To be successful, we must be good stewards of that which God has entrusted to us. This is the third principle of success. In the parable of the talents, we learn that God has given some five talents, others two, and still others only one. In the parable, the one given five talents gained five more and the one given two talents gained two more. The one given one talent dug a hole in the ground and buried it. On the day of accountability, God ordered the worthless slave, who did nothing, to be cast from His presence—and what he had had was given to those who were faithful with what had been entrusted to them.

God knows that we don't all have the same opportunities. Therefore, we will not be required to produce the same fruit. But He does require us to use what we have been given. Our potential for success does not lie in opportunity, but in faithfulness. What we want to hear is, "Well done, good and faithful slave; you were faithful with a few things, I will put you in charge of many things; enter into the joy of your master" (Matthew 25:21).

A Biblical Definition of Failure

In addition to being the authoritative Word of God, the Bible is a book of failures. Moses struck the rock in anger and failed to reach the promised land. Elijah killed 450 prophets of Baal, but ran from Queen Jezebel. David slew Goliath but also slept with Bathsheba and brought great pain on his family. Peter told the Lord to His face that he would go to prison and even be willing to die for Him, then he turned around and denied Him three times.

Even Jesus failed to accomplish what His disciples had hoped for, but He perfectly fulfilled His calling. Failure by our standards is not sin, but faithlessness is. Many of the heroes mentioned in Hebrews 11 would be considered failures by modern-day standards. But they weren't mentioned because of their accomplishments—they were commended for their faithfulness.

The book of Proverbs says, "A righteous man falls seven times, and rises again" (24:16). To stumble and fall is not failure. To stumble and fall again is not failure. Failure comes when you say, "I was pushed," and then fail to get up again. We have failed ourselves if we blame others for our lack of progress or rationalize why we can't get back up. We have failed others when we don't assume our responsibility in the body of Christ.

There are two kinds of failures: moral failure and failure to meet certain objectives. Moral failure cannot be blamed on anyone but ourselves. Such failure needs to be acknowledged only to the extent of the exposure and to those potentially affected by the sin. If only God knows, then confess only to Him unless others have been or could be affected by the sin. "If we confess our sins, He is faithful and righteous to forgive us our sins and to cleanse us from all unrighteousness. If we say that we have not sinned, we make Him a liar and His word is not in us" (1 John 1:9-10). So you have sinned. Confess it, get back up again, and keep moving forward. It is a moral failure to blame someone else or never acknowledge your sin to God. The opposite of confession is not only silence, but also rationalization.

Everybody has failed to accomplish his or her objectives at times. We have failed in the past, and we will fail tomorrow. A mistake is never a failure unless you fail to learn from it.

Many people who are afraid to fail never try—or they give up when they feel the slightest resistance. Failure is the line of least persistence. People don't fail; they give up trying. Success is 90 percent attitude and 10 percent aptitude. Those who accomplish something in their lives will look back and say it was persistence that got them there. Success is 10 percent inspiration and 90 percent perspiration.

Taking the Risk

Stepping out in faith is a risk, but *life* is a risk. We all like the security of the trunk, but the fruit is always out on the end of the limb. An anonymous author wrote,

> To *laugh* is to risk appearing the fool.
>
> To *weep* is to risk appearing sentimental.
>
> To *reach out* for another is to risk involvement.

To *expose feelings* to another is to risk exposing your true self.

To *place your ideas, your dreams* before a crowd is to risk their loss.

To *love* is to risk not being loved in return.

To *live* is to risk dying.

To *hope* is to risk despair.

To *try* is to risk failure.

But risks must be taken because the greatest hazard in life is to risk nothing. Those who risk nothing do nothing, have nothing, are nothing. They may avoid suffering and sorrow, but they simply cannot learn, feel, change, grow, love...live. Chained by the things they think are certain, they are slaves—they have forfeited freedom. Only people who risk are free.

If you were to make a list of the most offensive people in the world, who would be on the top of your list? Now compare it with the Lord's in Revelation 21:7-8:

> He who overcomes will inherit these things, and I will be his God and he will be My son. But for the cowardly and unbelieving and abominable and murderers and immoral persons and sorcerers and idolaters and all liars, their part will be in the lake that burns with fire and brimstone, which is the second death.

We would expect murderers, sorcerers, and idolaters to be on the list, but how many would guess that the list would be headed by cowardly and unbelieving? God does not look with favor on those who limp along in unbelief and never take the risk of living by faith because of fear of failure. It is the mark of a Spirit-filled Christian to be strong in the Lord and courageous.

When the early church was threatened, they turned to God in prayer, "and when they had prayed, the place where they had gathered together was shaken, and they were all filled with the Holy Spirit and began to speak the word of God with boldness" (Acts 4:31). "For God has not given us a spirit of timidity, but of power and love and discipline" (2 Timothy 1:7).

Feel the Fear, but Step Out Anyway

Susan Jeffers was raised to believe that she couldn't. Then one day this timid soul decided she wouldn't—no, she couldn't—live that way any longer. She writes,

> Part of my problem was the nonstop little voice inside my head that kept telling me, *You'd better not change your situation. There's nothing else out there for you. You'll never make it on your own.* You know the one I'm talking about—the one that keeps reminding you, *Don't take a chance. You might make a mistake. Boy, will you be sorry!*
>
> My fear never seemed to abate, and I didn't have a moment's peace. Then one day, as I was dressing for work, I reached the turning point. I happened to glance in the mirror, and I saw an all-too-familiar sight—eyes red and puffy from tears of self-pity. Suddenly rage welled up inside of me, and I began shouting at my reflection, "Enough…Enough…Enough!" I shouted until I had no more energy (or voice) left.
>
> When I stopped, I felt a strange and wonderful sense of relief and calm I had never felt before. Without realizing it at the time, I had gotten in touch with a very powerful part of myself that before that moment I hadn't even known ever existed. I took another look in the mirror and smiled as I nodded my head yes. The old familiar voice of doom and gloom was drowned out,

at least temporarily, and a new voice had come to the
fore—one that spoke of strength and love and joy and
all good things. At that moment I knew I was not going
to let fear get the best of me. I would find a way to rid
myself of the negativism that prevailed in my life. Thus
my adventure began. [2]

In her book *Feel the Fear and Do It Anyway,* Susan shares two
fundamental truths about fear. First, "the fear will never go away
as long as you continue to grow." Every step in our maturing
process will be met with new challenges and obstacles to overcome. You can't wait until the fear goes away, because it never
will—which leads to the second truth: "The only way to get rid
of the fear of doing something is to go out and do it."[3] Someone
once said, "Do the thing you fear the most and the death of fear
is certain."

Remember, nobody can keep you from being the person God
has called you to be. It is normal to feel the fear—but step out
anyway, as the following poem suggests:

> People are unreasonable, illogical, and self-centered.
> *Love them anyway.*
>
> If you do good, people will accuse you of selfish ulterior
> motives.
> *Do good anyway.*
>
> If you are successful, you will win false friends and true
> enemies.
> *Succeed anyway.*
>
> The good you do today will be forgotten tomorrow.
> *Do good anyway.*
>
> Honesty and frankness make you vulnerable.
> *Be honest and frank anyway.*

The biggest men and women with the biggest ideas can be shot down by the smallest men and women with the smallest minds.

Think big anyway.

People favor underdogs but follow only top dogs.
Fight for a few underdogs anyway.

What you spend years building may be destroyed overnight.
Build anyway.

People really need help but may attack you if you do help them.
Help people anyway.

Give the world the best you have, and you'll get kicked in the teeth.
Give the world the best you have anyway. [4]

Stomping Out Fear

Read:

Jeremiah 9:23-24

Reflect:

How does the world define success? How does the Bible define success? What are the three principles of success that are outlined in this chapter?

How do faith and faithfulness relate to success? How do they relate to failure?

List three or more things that you would like to attempt that you have previously put on hold because of fear of failure. What two principles did we learn from Susan Jeffers' book *Feel the Fear and Do It Anyway*? How do these principles relate to the things on your personal list?

Have you forgiven yourself for your failures—both your moral failures and your failures to reach an objective? How does 1 John 1:9-10 relate to this question?

Respond:

Dear heavenly Father, Your Word tells us that "a righteous man falls seven times, and rises again." I thank You that in Christ I have been declared righteous and that I am totally clean in Your eyes. Therefore I know that when I fall or fail, You will lift me up. I confess that I have sometimes feared failing and even stopped doing the very things I know that You have called me to do. I renounce the fear of failure, and I declare that in Christ I am free to try—and even fail— because I know You love me and will lift me up again and again. So I will endeavor to do my best, but I will depend on You and Your strength. In Jesus' name I pray, amen.

(See Proverbs 24:16.)

Overcoming Panic Attacks

> I did not realize I had a problem with fear until I had two surgeries in a short period of time. What a scary time that was for me. All I knew was that I wanted people praying for me. My prayer consisted of "Help, God."
>
> I became agitated and shaky inside. My chest began to tighten, and as time went by I would wake up every morning at three o'clock with crippling fear. It was as though my thoughts were out of control. I began to have rushes go through my body, and then I would collapse in tears.

PANIC ATTACKS (SOMETIMES CALLED ANXIETY ATTACKS) are defined in the *Baker Encyclopedia of Psychology* as "very frightening experiences in which persons are overwhelmed with the physical symptoms of anxiety."[1] Those symptoms generally include some of the following: "racing heartbeat, difficulty breathing—feeling as though you can't get enough air, terror that is almost paralyzing, dizziness, lightheadedness, nausea, trembling, shaking, sweating, choking, chest pains, hot flashes or sudden chills, tingling in fingers or toes like 'pins and needles,' fear that you are having a heart attack or that you are going crazy or about to die."[2]

These symptoms are similar to the "fight or flight" body responses to extreme stress and danger. They can occur suddenly, without warning, in seemingly harmless situations. They can even occur while an individual is sleeping,[3] as the story at the beginning of the chapter reveals.

If panic attacks occur frequently (one or more times during any four-week period) and involve at least four of the above symptoms, then the person's affliction is called *panic disorder.*[4] About 75 percent of panic disorder sufferers are women. It usually has its onset between the ages of 20 and 30, although it can first show up in teenage years or in adults over 40.

Although the first panic attack may come during a time of unusual stress, victims of this problem are often average, emotionally healthy people. The attacks typically reach maximum intensity within one or two minutes from their start and may last (with slowly diminishing symptoms) from 30 minutes to several hours.[5]

It is not uncommon for people, after suffering a number of panic episodes, to become increasingly afraid that they are helpless victims of panic. They may start avoiding public places and remain at home whenever possible. They become more apprehensive and tense, continually guarding against the possibility of another attack.[6] This fearful, defensive posture causes them to be even more susceptible to panic attacks. Nonetheless, many people with panic disorder still manage to muddle their way through life, coping as best they can.

The fear of having a panic attack causes many people to become agoraphobic. Agoraphobia (literally, "fear of the marketplace") can become so severe that sufferers may quit their jobs, stop going to church or youth group, avoid grocery stores and malls, and even dread talking on the telephone. In extreme cases, a person can become housebound for years.[7] Because the symptoms accompanying a panic attack can come without warning, agoraphobics literally become afraid of fear itself.

Our Adequacy Is in Christ

We feel anxious when what we think we need exceeds what we think we have. We panic when we feel helpless and out of control.

One of the goals of secular therapy is to convince people that they are adequate in themselves to handle their panic attacks. They have no other choice, but the apostle Paul advocates a different answer for the Christian: "Not that we are adequate in ourselves to consider anything as coming from ourselves, but our adequacy is from God, who also made us adequate as servants of a new covenant" (2 Corinthians 3:5-6).

As children of God, we have entered into a new covenant, or promise-keeping relationship, with our heavenly Father. In the flesh we are weak and helpless, but "in Christ" we can do all things through Him who strengthens us (Philippians 4:13). In the flesh we may lose control, but if we walk by the Spirit we will have self-control (Galatians 5:23). "A natural man does not accept the things of the Spirit of God…but we have the mind of Christ" (1 Corinthians 2:14,16). For these reasons, as we've talked about before, Jesus instructs us to

> seek first His kingdom and His righteousness; and all these things will be added to you. So do not worry about tomorrow; for tomorrow will care for itself. Each day has enough trouble of its own (Matthew 6:33-34).

There is one other important spiritual factor that must be considered. Paul says,

> Do you not know that your bodies are members of Christ?…Do you not know that your body is a temple of the Holy Spirit who is in you, whom you have from

God, and that you are not your own? For you have been
bought with a price: therefore glorify God in your body
(1 Corinthians 6:15,19-20).

Our bodies are not our own. We, including our bodies, belong
to God. So we need to be good stewards of our bodies and submit
them to Him as living sacrifices (Romans 12:1).

Renewing the Mind

The origin of a panic attack can be a signal to our brain from our
physical bodies saying something is wrong. How we interpret that
signal is dependent upon how our minds have been previously
programmed and what we presently think and believe. (The
origin of a panic attack can also be a spiritual battle for our
minds, which we'll talk more about later.)

The central nervous system regulates every body function
according to how the mind has been programmed. Beyond getting proper medical help when needed, we need to be transformed by the renewing of our minds. The purpose of *cognitive
therapy* is to help sufferers understand how their panic is the result
of how they think and what they believe. You don't do anything
or feel anything without first thinking something. The emotional response of fear is *always* preceded by a thought, although
it can be so rapid that you're hardly aware of the connection.

Personalities and patterns of thinking have been developed
over time, and it takes time to renew the mind. In particular, there
are several personalities that are more vulnerable to anxiety and
panic.

The Worrier

Worriers find it hard to rest in the loving and protective arms of
their heavenly Father. They feel that life's problems present a
clear and present danger that calls for continual vigilance on

their part, lest they be caught off guard. For instance, at a "fear of flying school," the students were asked if they thought their worrying would help keep the plane in the air. Everyone agreed they had such thoughts.

Maybe that is why Jesus asked, "Who of you by being worried can add a single hour to his life?" (Matthew 6:27). The answer is no one, but you can seriously reduce the number of your life's hours by worrying. Isaiah has strong words of comfort to those who put their trust in the Lord, and a sobering word of warning for those who don't:

> Thus the Lord GOD, the Holy One of Israel, has said, "In repentance and rest you will be saved, in quietness and trust is your strength." But you were not willing, and you said, "No, for we will flee on horses," therefore you will flee! "And we will ride on swift horses," therefore those who pursue you shall be swift. One thousand will flee at the threat of one man; you will flee at the threat of five, until you are left as a flag on a mountain top and as a signal on a hill.

> Therefore the LORD longs to be gracious to you, and therefore He waits on high to have compassion on you. For the LORD is a God of justice; how blessed are all those who long for Him (Isaiah 30:15-18).

The Victim

The "victim" is overwhelmed by a sense of helplessness and hopelessness. But the whole message of the cross is that Jesus became the victim so that we can be victors in Him. Though the world may have dealt us a bad hand, we can still be overcomers. "Whatever is born of God overcomes the world; and this is the victory that has overcome the world—our faith. Who is the one who overcomes the world, but he who believes that Jesus is the Son of God?" (1 John 5:4-5).

We overcome the world because Jesus has already done so. We enter into that victory by believing the truth. The person who is convinced that he or she is helpless or hopeless has believed a lie and is consequently unable to walk by faith.

But how can we be helpless when the Bible says we can do all things through Christ who strengthens us (see Philippians 4:13)? How can we be hopeless when the God of hope is in us and He is able to fill us with all joy and peace in believing, that we may abound in hope by the power of the Holy Spirit (see Romans 15:13)?

Playing the role of the victim can become an excuse for not getting well. Jesus encountered such a man one day in Jerusalem:

> Now there is in Jerusalem by the sheep gate a pool, which is called in Hebrew Bethesda, having five porticoes. In these lay a multitude of those who were sick, blind, lame, and withered, [waiting for the moving of the waters; for an angel of the Lord went down at certain seasons into the pool and stirred up the water; whoever then first, after the stirring up of the water, stepped in was made well from whatever disease with which he was afflicted.]

> A man was there who had been ill for thirty-eight years. When Jesus saw him lying there, and knew that he had already been a long time in that condition, He said to him, "Do you wish to get well?"

> The sick man answered Him, "Sir, I have no man to put me into the pool when the water is stirred up, but while I am coming, another steps down before me."

> Jesus said to him, "Get up, pick up your pallet and walk."

> Immediately the man became well, and picked up his pallet and began to walk (John 5:2-9, brackets in original).

"Do you wish to get well?" That is not a cruel question; it is a very important one. You can't get well unless you desire it and are willing to make the commitment to do whatever it takes. All of us have been victimized, and we can't promise that you won't be again. But we can promise you that you don't have to remain a victim for the rest of your life. Nobody can fix the past. Even God doesn't do that. But we can be free from it by the grace of God. That wonderful truth is inherent in the gospel.

The Critic

Another pattern is the "critic." Their oversensitive conscience berates themselves and others. They come under mental attack by an unrelenting barrage of thoughts like "I can't do anything right." "I am so stupid." "Other people don't struggle with this, but look at me!" Critics never feel good about themselves or what they have done. They are discouraged and defeated even before the panic attack hits.

Often echoing the voices of demanding parents, teachers, coaches, or employers, critics' inner voices slap negative labels on their souls, hindering them from experiencing the joy and freedom of being children of God. Faith is drained away, and they feel constantly put down for not being able to overcome their fears and live a normal life.

Closely related to critics are perfectionists. They never have any peace of mind because they can never achieve perfection. Their overwhelming need to accomplish more and more makes them driven, stressed, and irritable. They are setting themselves up for an anxiety disorder because they can't stand to fail, especially in public.

The Spiritual Battle for the Mind

What brings on panic attacks in the first place? What causes a person who is normally able to handle stress to suddenly be stricken with one? Why do people sometimes awaken terrorized from a sound sleep? And why do Christians often find instantaneous freedom from these attacks when they call upon the name of the Lord? These burning questions were on the mind of someone who contacted our ministry:

> I am wondering if you can help me out with a particular experience that has plagued me and my sleep for the past six or seven years. Although I am a Christian, I have probably experienced about 15 of these panic attacks over the past several years.
>
> They are usually associated with a time in which I've given something over to God or committed my ways to Him.
>
> Here is a little history about my sleeping habits. When I was young I would dream very intense dreams about spirits or things related to the spirit world. I'm not sure why, except that I am an artist and have always had a very vivid imagination. Other nights I would dream about the end times and things that would happen— very intense dreams also!
>
> As I got older these dreams would happen less frequently, but when they did come they came with the same intensity.
>
> When I turned 17, I received a calling from God— a very distinct one. Unfortunately, because of my pride and fear, I did not follow that calling. Through the years since then I have received many opportunities to follow that original calling, and each time I tried the panic attack would result. Consequently, I would back off from the calling because of the fear of another attack.
>
> The panic attack usually starts by waking me out of my sleep to either a rushing sound in my ear, many people talking incoherently, or many people screaming.

By the time this ends (usually in about 5 or 10 seconds) an intense, indescribable, mammoth fear envelops my whole body.

I really can't describe how intense this fear is. My body becomes physically paralyzed—no movement. I can't talk. I can move my eyes around and can hear, though. Finally a heavy weight seems to rest on my chest and pushes me into my bed. At least that's what it feels like.

This whole experience lasts about a minute, but then I am usually wide awake and scared. I'm not sure what causes this, but I think it may be demonic.

We think so, too. The fact that these attacks occurred around the time this woman was making a serious move toward God could indicate a spiritual attack. Unfortunately, the scare tactic worked. She backed off from obeying God because of the fear. This is a very common strategy of the enemy. When I first started conducting conferences, I experienced the same kind of attack every evening before a conference would begin. (You begin to wonder about yourself since nobody ever talks about these experiences in most of our churches.)

So I began to ask during the conferences, "How many people have had the following experience: You were suddenly awakened from a sound sleep with a tremendous sense of fear. You tried to move or say something, but you couldn't. You possibly felt a pressure on your chest or something grabbing your throat." At least a third of the attendees in every conference have had at least one such experience sometime in their lives.

Most of these people have never shared their experiences. If people did share these experiences with secular counselors, those counselors would likely call them panic attacks. They don't call them "fear attacks," because they can't identify the object of the fear. We can! This is a spiritual attack, and it can be resolved very easily.

Our Response to an Attack

The natural response to fear is to say or do something immediately. Then why couldn't we simply physically respond? Because we cannot resolve the problem physically. The Bible says, "Though we live in the world, we do not wage war as the world does. The weapons we fight with are not the weapons of the world. On the contrary, they have divine power to demolish strongholds" (2 Corinthians 10:3-4 NIV).

God knows the thoughts and intentions of our heart, so we can always call upon the Lord in our minds. The moment we do, we will be able to speak. All we have to say is "Jesus," and the devil will flee: "At the name of Jesus every knee will bow, in heaven and on earth and under the earth" (Philippians 2:10 NLT). The order of Scripture is critical. First, submit to God inwardly, and then you will be able to resist the devil outwardly (James 4:7).

Spiritual attacks usually occur at night when we are alone and more vulnerable. Being awakened out of a sound sleep heightens our sense of terror. We are caught off guard and easily confused. Scripture is filled with examples of humans being overwhelmed with fear in the presence of spiritual beings. Job's friend, Eliphaz, described an experience he had:

> Now a word was brought to me stealthily, and my ear received a whisper of it. Amid disquieting thoughts from the visions of the night, when deep sleep falls on men, dread came upon me, and trembling, and made all my bones shake. Then a spirit passed by my face; the hair of my flesh bristled up. It stood still, but I could not discern its appearance; a form was before my eyes (Job 4:12-16).

The prophet Daniel and his companions were visited by a powerful heavenly messenger and experienced symptoms not unlike those of a panic attack:

> I, Daniel, alone saw the vision, while the men who were with me did not see the vision; nevertheless, a great dread fell on them, and they ran away to hide themselves. So I was left alone and saw this great vision; yet no strength was left in me, for my natural color turned to a deathly pallor, and I retained no strength (Daniel 10:7-8).

Several times Daniel was so debilitated by this vision that the angel had to encourage him by saying, "Do not be afraid," and touched him physically so that he could be strengthened. Daniel's description of how this angelic encounter affected his breathing is particularly significant in light of the symptoms of panic attacks we discussed earlier. "How can such a servant of my lord talk with such as my lord? As for me, there remains just now no strength in me, nor has any breath been left in me" (Daniel 10:17).

The point of all this? We must realize that the Bible teaches that at times the presence or appearance of angels causes great fear to fall on people, though not always. It is then completely consistent with Scripture to say that a fallen angel (demon), if it chose to do so, could manifest itself to a human being and cause tremendous fear. At other times one could pay attention to a deceiving spirit or spirit guide, thinking it was a friend.

Discernment Is Needed

How can we discern what is from God? The Bible says,

> Humble yourselves under the mighty hand of God, that He may exalt you at the proper time, casting all your anxiety on Him, because He cares for you. Be of sober spirit,

be on the alert. Your adversary, the devil, prowls around
like a roaring lion, seeking someone to devour (1 Peter
5:6-8).

Lions roar in order to paralyze their prey with fear so they can
consume them. Sometimes they will stand over a little burrow and
roar. Some little animal will come running out in fear, right into
the jaws of death.

But this lion doesn't have any teeth. The devil is defeated and
disarmed. All he can do is roar. But his lying demons are paralyzing young people in fear. We cannot escape the biblical connection between anxiety (double-mindedness) and the spiritual
battle for our minds. We can also see the connection in Ephesians
4:25-27: "Laying aside falsehood, speak truth each one of you with
his neighbor, for we are members of one another. Be angry, and
yet do not sin; do not let the sun go down on your anger, and do
not give the devil an opportunity."

We have been clearly warned. "The Spirit explicitly says that
in later times some will fall away from the faith, paying attention
to deceitful spirits and doctrines of demons" (1 Timothy 4:1). Paul
says, "I am afraid that, as the serpent deceived Eve by his craftiness, your minds will be led astray from the simplicity and purity
of devotion to Christ" (2 Corinthians 11:3).

Choose the Truth

To win this battle for our minds we must take every thought captive to the obedience of Christ. It doesn't make any difference if
the thoughts in our minds come from our memory, the Internet,
another person, hell itself, or are original thoughts of our own.
We take *every* thought captive. If what we are thinking isn't true
according to the Word of God, then we shouldn't believe it.

Should we rebuke every negative thought? No! You don't
overcome the father of lies by trying not to believe him. You

overcome the lies of this world by choosing the truth, and you keep choosing it until your mind is renewed. If you think you are going to panic, you probably will. If you believe in your heart that all things are possible with Christ and that you can do all things through Him who strengthens you, then you can. Whether you think you can or whether you think you can't, either way you are right, "for as he thinks within himself, so he is" (Proverbs 23:7).

The enemies of our sanctification are the world, the flesh, and the devil. There are definite dangers in this world, but Jesus said, "In the world you have tribulation, but take courage; I have overcome the world" (John 16:33). Our flesh is in opposition to the Spirit, but "those who belong to Christ Jesus have crucified the flesh with its passions and desires" (Galatians 5:24). The devil is roaring around like a lion, but you are not alone in your struggle. Peter's advice is to "resist him, firm in your faith, knowing that the same experiences of suffering are being accomplished by your brethren who are in the world" (1 Peter 5:9). Be encouraged by what Jesus said:

> Peace I leave with you; My peace I give to you; not as the world gives do I give to you. Do not let your heart be troubled, nor let it be fearful (John 14:27).

Stomping Out Fear

Read:
1 John 5:4-5

Reflect:
What are panic or anxiety attacks? What are the symptoms?

Secular therapy tries to convince people they're adequate in themselves to handle panic attacks. Why isn't this very practical, and what does the Bible say about how adequate we are without Christ? In what ways *are* we adequate in Christ? Check out 2 Corinthians 3:5-6.

Explain what the "fear of fear" is and how it relates to panic attacks. How do anxiety attacks relate to our personality, like the "worrier" or "critic"? Why is it so important to take every thought captive? Check out 2 Corinthians 10:5.

Respond:
Dear heavenly Father, I confess that I have at times listened to the devil's roaring. I know that he parades around like a lion. However, this toothless lion has been disarmed by Jesus the Christ. I know now that I am not alone in my struggle. I choose to take Peter's advice and resist Satan and stand firm in my faith. I know that I am no different than other believers and that they are experiencing the same suffering. I choose to walk in the peace that Jesus offered every believer when He said, "Peace I leave with you; My peace I give to you; not as the world gives do I give to you. Do not let your heart be troubled, nor let it be fearful." So, I here and now reject fear and embrace peace. In Jesus' name I pray, amen.

(See 1 Peter 5:9; John 14:27.)

Breaking Strongholds of Fear

Seven

THE FOLLOWING ACCOUNT WAS A REAL REMINDER to me (Rich) of the power of fear to control. But more than that, it serves as a demonstration of the tender mercy and grace of God to deliver a child from fear.

"Brian has been acting a little strange lately," my wife, Shirley, remarked once the kids had left the room. I could tell she was concerned. I had just returned from a ministry trip and was getting the usual "state of the family" update.

"In what way?" I replied, putting down the mail I was sorting through. I was concerned, too, since our then five-year-old son seemed to be vulnerable at times.

"Well, he hasn't wanted to eat anything sweet for a few days. And when he was over at a friend's house, he wouldn't even eat ice cream. At least not until they told him there wasn't any sugar in it." She chuckled a little bit at their success in tricking Brian.

"It sounds like he's afraid of eating sugar. Have they had a dental hygienist or somebody like that at preschool lately?"

There had been someone talking about "sugar bugs" in his class recently, and that had apparently scared him. We decided to wait and see what happened. That night after dinner, Brian refused the cookie that the others got and opted instead for a banana.

"You know, Brian, bananas have sugar in them, too. Natural sugar. It's good for you. In fact, just about everything these days has sugar in it. So to keep from eating sugar, you'd have to stop eating!" I laughed as I finished my "inspired" sermon, fully expecting that Brian would laugh with me and chomp down the banana. I turned back to washing the dishes in the sink, figuring that this was the end of this fear-of-sugar nonsense. The whole thing seemed rather silly. After all, most parents would be overjoyed if their five-year-old stopped eating sugary foods!

A minute or so later, I caught a movement out of the corner of my eye. It didn't register at first, but then I realized that it was Brian. I turned around to see that he was gone from the kitchen table and so was his dessert. I looked in the trash can and there was the uneaten banana.

A little annoyed at Brian's self-will, I marched upstairs to his room. He was sitting on his bed in tears. Softening a bit upon seeing how upset he was, I asked him, "What's wrong, Brian? Why didn't you eat the banana?"

"It has sugar in it." Frustrated by the irrationality of the whole thing, I left his room, went downstairs and picked up a banana. I took it up to his room, a "brilliant" plan unfolding in my mind.

"Brian, there's nothing to be afraid of. Watch what I do." Breaking the banana in half, I gave one part to him and kept the other. "Daddy is going to eat half of the banana, and you eat the other half, okay?"

He wasn't impressed. As I enthusiastically wolfed down my half, he gingerly took a microscopic bite and promptly spat it out. By that time, I was really frustrated but still undaunted. Another plan formulated itself in my mind. I went back to the kitchen and grabbed a candy bar. *There's no way he'll be able to resist that,* I reasoned.

I was wrong! As I chomped down my half, he just stared blankly at me, holding his end of the bargain like it was a mildewed brussels sprout. At wit's end, I slunk downstairs to find Shirley. Totally exasperated, I finally got around to doing what I should have done in the first place.

"Shirley, we need to pray. Brian's fear of sugar is real and serious. Something is very wrong. He wouldn't even eat the candy bar I gave him."

As we prayed, I confessed my frustration. God's peace returned. So did wisdom! The Lord clearly directed me to go back and pray with Brian, seeking the root of his problem, just as I would with an adult.

The Lord moved, and Brian was much calmer. He was able to recall some of the things that had scared him. One by one he, in his five-year-old way, renounced those fears: "I say no to the fear of _____!" Heights, fire, bad dreams, and a few other typical childhood fears came to our minds.

Happy for the progress we had made, I was still perplexed as to why he was so fearful of sweets.

"Brian, why are you so afraid of eating sugar?"

"'Cause I'll get a cavity," he answered, choking back the tears.

"No, you won't. We'll brush your teeth, and that won't be a problem at all."

I could tell he still was not convinced. "Brian, do you know what a cavity is?"

He shook his head, tears starting to roll down his cheeks. I then hoped that my clear explanation of the nature, origin, and treatment of cavities would do the trick. No dice. So I prayed for more wisdom, and God brought the first breakthrough we needed to help Brian overcome his fear.

"Brian, what do you think will happen to you if you get a cavity?" I asked, sensing that something critical was about to be revealed.

"I'll die." Bingo! The poor kid had believed the lie that sugar = cavity = death. No wonder he was so afraid of sugar! He had likely misinterpreted something that had been said in his school.

I had Brian renounce the fear of cavities, the fear of death, and also the spirit of fear, affirming that God had not given that to him. He announced that God had instead given him power, love, and a sound mind.

But that wasn't the end of the battle. In school the next day he hardly touched his peanut-butter-and-jelly sandwich. Shirley and I prayed again, this time personally dealing with any fears that we and our parents could have passed on to our children. The Lord then led us to help Brian face his fear head on. The showdown was to be that evening after dinner—at the local Dairy Queen.

I could tell that Brian was nervous after we told him where we were going for dessert. "I'm not hungry for any dessert," he lied, hoping we would leave him alone.

Upon arrival, I purchased everyone's ice cream, including a vanilla cone (his favorite at the time) for Brian. He watched in silence as everyone else ferociously attacked their dessert. I pointed out to him that his sisters, Michelle and Emily, as well as his mommy and daddy were all eating ice cream. And none of us was getting a cavity. Obviously, none of us had dropped dead. Still his dessert sat, rivulets of melted ice cream forming small puddles on the table. The "girls" all finished theirs and headed to the rest room. I felt like I had to press the issue to a crisis point with my son.

"Brian, I know you are thinking that if you eat anything with sugar in it, you will die. There's only one way you'll ever know if that little thought in your head is the truth or a lie."

"What's that?" he asked, turning his sad eyes toward me.

"Take a bite." Rarely have I prayed so fervently. And rarely have I felt such joy as when he leaned over and took a bite.

Relieved, I said quietly, "Did you get a cavity?"

"No," Brian replied, the faintest smile appearing on his face.

"And did you die?" I asked, grinning from ear to ear.

"No." By this time, Brian was smiling, too.

"Then take another bite."

Thankfully, he did. And then he took another and another and another, without any coaxing from me. And then he turned and said something I'll always remember:

"Daddy, I just felt the fear inside of me snap in two, just like a stick."

And it was over. Really over. Not only was the fear broken, but the lie behind it was overcome by truth. Before that incident Brian had been very fearful. Now he is not afraid at all. Despite his small size, he is one of the happiest, most confident boys you would want to meet. A wide grin rarely leaves his face.

Some Important Cautions

There are two reasons why we shared that rather lengthy "home movie." First, to show you what is *not* effective in dealing with a stronghold of fear. Second, this story provides a helpful illustration of breaking down the walls of fear—one that we will draw upon when we explain the "Fear Finder."

The futility of trying to resolve an anxiety disorder with mere human reasoning is obvious. In the heat of battle our own ideas can appear quite clever. The temptation is to lean on our own understanding rather than trusting in the Lord with all our hearts. The Lord promises to make our paths straight when we acknowledge Him in all our ways (Proverbs 3:5-6).We need the guidance of God to find the root cause of fear and the grace of God to overcome it.

Many of the struggles we have are simply a matter of growth and are better left to the healing power of time. But we cannot assume that every strange or unusual behavior in our lives is just a phase that we will outgrow. Debilitating problems like paranoia, lying, abusive behavior, and rebellion have to be resolved. The Lord will give discernment to those who truly seek it, providing the wisdom to know His path to freedom and healing. The human soul and spirit are remarkably complex, but we have this promise about God's Word:

> The word of God is living and active and sharper than any two-edged sword, and piercing as far as the division

of soul and spirit, of both joints and marrow, and able to judge the thoughts and intentions of the heart. And there is no creature hidden from His sight, but all things are open and laid bare to the eyes of Him with whom we have to do (Hebrews 4:12-13).

James provides the biblical basis for finding and maintaining freedom from fear:

He gives a greater grace. Therefore it says, "God is opposed to the proud, but gives grace to the humble." Submit therefore to God. Resist the devil and he will flee from you. Draw near to God and He will draw near to you (James 4:6-8).

The Key to Freedom

We need to stop submitting to fear and start submitting to God. The word *submit* means to subject oneself to some authority. It was a military term meaning to rank or arrange under. Submitting means letting go of the reins and putting them in the hands of someone who is superior in rank. To submit to God is to come under His authority. It is to acknowledge the presence and power of our heavenly Father. We are acknowledging Him as the only legitimate fear object when we submit to Him. The essence of humility is to "put no confidence in the flesh" and choose to "be strong in the LORD and in the strength of His might" (see Philippians 3:3; Ephesians 6:10).

This beginning step of freedom from fear may be the most frightening part of the process for some people, as with the boy who slipped at the edge of a cliff, but managed to hang on to a tree branch for dear life. He could not pull himself up, and to lose his grip on the branch meant sudden death. He cried for help, and to his relief he heard a voice say, "I will help you."

The desperate boy looked up but didn't see anybody. "Who are you?" he asked. "Are you going to help me?"

Then he heard the voice say, "I'm the one who created you, and I will help you because I love you—but you have to let go!"

There was a long silence. Finally the boy yelled, "Help! Help! Is Anyone else up there?"

That is the step of faith that all of us must take in order to be saved. What alternative do we have? We can try to save ourselves, but eventually we will lose our grip and fall. If hanging on to the reins of our own life has only resulted in fear and anxiety thus far, does that not clearly reveal the futility of such a choice? Could not the presence of anxiety be the very motivation we need in order to submit to God and experience His peace? We have to be brought to the end of our self-sufficiency in order to find our sufficiency in Christ.

True Versus False Security

It is far safer to put ourselves into the hands of our all-sufficient heavenly Father than to rely on the false security that comes from relying on our own resources. As God's children we have not been left as orphans—but many Christians live as if they have no heavenly Father at all (see John 14:18). Does the prospect of letting go of control of your life scare you?

We urge you to let go and make a good start by going through the Steps to Freedom in Christ in the back of this book. It is a thorough spiritual and moral inventory. If possible, work through them with a youth pastor, counselor, or Christian friend you trust and can be open and honest with.

The Steps to Freedom are a guide, not a formula. Only Jesus can set us free, but the Steps have been a helpful tool for thousands of young people who want to experience the freedom Christ purchased for them at Calvary. The Steps will help you resolve personal and spiritual conflicts by submitting to God and resisting the devil.

Seek God First

We cannot overstate how necessary it is to get right with God first. David wrote,

> I sought the LORD, and He answered me, and delivered me from all my fears. They looked to Him and were radiant, and their faces will never be ashamed. This poor man cried, and the LORD heard him and saved him out of all his troubles. The angel of the LORD encamps around those who fear Him, and rescues them (Psalm 34:4-7).

This was a lesson that Joshua had to learn the hard way. Fresh off their awesome victory over Jericho, Joshua and the Israelites set their sights on the next conquest. The small town of Ai appeared weak compared to the mighty walled city that had just fallen before them. So Joshua dispatched a team of men to spy out the land.

The spies came back confident that only a few thousand men would be needed to take Ai. Joshua listened to their counsel, but neglected to inquire of God. As a result, the small Israelite army was soundly defeated, and 36 men lost their lives.

Joshua, being a godly man at heart, fell down before the Lord in mourning. He complained to Him about the defeat, their humiliation, and even the damage done to the great name of God. Joshua was paralyzed by fear and discouragement and uncertain as to what he should do next. God responded by saying,

> Rise up! Consecrate the people and say, "Consecrate yourselves for tomorrow, for thus the LORD, the God of Israel, has said, 'There are things under the ban in your midst, O Israel. You cannot stand before your enemies

until you have removed the things under the ban from your midst'" (Joshua 7:13).

STEPS TO STOMPING OUT FEAR

If you have successfully resolved your personal and spiritual conflicts by submitting to God and resisting the devil, then you are ready to analyze, or stomp out, your fears and work out a responsible course of action. To do so, use the following "Fear Finder":

Fear Finder

A. Analyze your fear under God's authority and guidance.

1. Identify all fear objects (what are you afraid of?).

2. Determine when you first experienced the fear.

3. What events preceded the first experience?

4. Determine the lies behind every phobia.

B. Determine the ways you have been living under the control of fear rather than living by faith in God.

1. How has fear

a. prevented you from doing what is right and responsible?

b. compelled you to do what is wrong and irresponsible?

c. prompted you to compromise your witness for Christ?

2. Confess any active or passive way in which you have allowed fear to control your life.

3. Commit yourself to God to live a righteous and responsible life.

C. Prayerfully work out a plan of responsible behavior.

D. Determine in advance what your response will be to any fear object.

E. Commit yourself to carry out your plan of action in the power of the Holy Spirit.[1]

Analyze Your Fear

Begin the first step in the "Fear Finder" by praying the following prayer out loud:

> *Dear heavenly Father, I come to You as Your child. I put myself under Your awesome and powerful care and I know that You are the only legitimate fear object in my life. I confess that I have been fearful and anxious because of my lack of trust and my unbelief. I have not always lived by faith in You, and too often I have relied on my own strength and resources. I thank You that I am forgiven in Christ.*
>
> *I choose to believe the truth that You have not given me a spirit of fear, but of power, love, and a sound mind. Therefore, I renounce any spirit of fear. I ask You to reveal to my mind all the fears that have been controlling me. Show me how I have become fearful and the lies I have believed. I desire to live a responsible life in the power of Your Holy Spirit. Show me how these fears have kept me from doing that. I ask this so that I can confess, renounce, and overcome every fear by faith in You. In Jesus' name I pray, amen.*

The following list may help you recognize some of the fears that have been hindering your walk of faith. On the page or on a separate sheet, write down the ones that apply to you, as well as any others not on the list that the Spirit of God has revealed to you. As you prayerfully recall your past, write a brief description of what happened (and when) to trigger that fear.

- ❏ Fear of Satan
- ❏ Fear of parents getting a divorce
- ❏ Fear of death
- ❏ Fear of not being loved by God
- ❏ Fear of never being loved
- ❏ Fear of not being able to love others
- ❏ Fear of rejection by people
- ❏ Fear of disapproval
- ❏ Fear of embarrassment
- ❏ Fear of failure
- ❏ Fear of being or becoming homosexual
- ❏ Fear of financial problems
- ❏ Fear of going crazy
- ❏ Fear of being a hopeless case
- ❏ Fear of the death of a loved one
- ❏ Fear of the future
- ❏ Fear of confrontation
- ❏ Fear of being victimized by crime
- ❏ Fear of losing my salvation
- ❏ Fear of committing the unpardonable sin

❒ Fear of specific people, animals, or objects

❒ Other specific fears the Lord brings to mind:

We all live by faith, but the real question is, "What or whom do we believe?" You could choose to believe that it would be hopeless to even try overcoming your fears. But that's not true. God is the God of all hope, and there is nothing that is too difficult for Him (see Romans 15:13; Jeremiah 32:17).

You could choose to believe that it is safer and wiser to avoid certain strong-willed people, or elevators, or airplanes. You could believe, like Rich's son did, that sugar in foods will kill you. Such false beliefs are not neutral or harmless, because whatever is not of faith is sin (Romans 14:23). *The root of any phobia is a belief that is not based in truth.* These false beliefs need to be uprooted and replaced by the truth of God's Word.

Take as much time in prayer as you need to discern these lies because renouncing them and choosing the truth is a critical step toward gaining and maintaining your freedom in Christ. Search the Scriptures for the truth. Seek counsel from your youth pastor or other mature, godly believers. You have to know and choose to believe the truth in order for it to set you free. Write down the lies you have believed for every fear and the corresponding truth from the Word of God.

Analyzing Your Lifestyle

The next step is to determine how fear has prevented you from living a responsible life, compelled you to do that which is irresponsible, or compromised your Christian witness. Phobias affect how we live, and we need to know how they have done this.

For instance, a teenager may compromise his faith and participate in a crime because he is afraid his friends will reject him.

After you have taken time to seek the Lord on these matters and you feel you have gained the necessary insights into your fear, it is time to experience God's cleansing through confession and repentance: "If we confess our sins, He is faithful and righteous to forgive us our sins and to cleanse us from all unrighteousness" (1 John 1:9; see also Proverbs 28:13). Remember, it is the kindness of God that leads you to repentance (Romans 2:4). Confession is agreeing with God that what you did was sinful. Repentance is the choice to turn away from sin and walk by faith in God.

Say the following prayer for each of the controlling fears that you have discovered above:

> *Dear Lord, I now confess and repent of the fear of _____ . I have believed (<u>state the lie</u>). I renounce that lie, and I choose to believe the truth (<u>state the truth</u>). I also confess any and all ways this fear has resulted in my living irresponsibly or compromising my witness for Christ, including _____ .*
>
> *I now choose to live by faith in You, Lord, believing Your promise that You will protect me and meet all my needs. In Jesus' trustworthy name I pray, amen.*

After working through every fear the Lord has revealed to you (including their accompanying lies and sinful behavior), pray the following prayer:

> *Dear heavenly Father, I thank You that You are indeed trustworthy. I choose to believe You even when my feelings and circumstances tell me to fear. You have told me not to fear, for You are with me; to not anxiously look about me, for You are my God. You will strengthen me, help me, and surely uphold me with Your righteous right hand.*

I now ask You to show me Your plan of action for living responsibly and facing my fear. I commit myself to do what You tell me to do, knowing that Your grace is sufficient. I pray this with faith in the name of Jesus, my Savior and Lord, amen.

Most of the lies we have believed come from living in a fallen world, but the god of this world is the father of lies (John 8:44). Part of the purpose of encouraging you to go through the Steps to Freedom in Christ and to use the "Fear Finder" to analyze your fears is so you can understand what part the devil may be playing in your struggle with fear and anxiety. That is precisely what happened to this person:

Having only been a Christian for five years, I was just coming to understand that many of my experiences of fear and anxiety were not of God, but were of Satan. I couldn't drive over bridges without feeling like I was going to lose control of the steering wheel. I could see myself and my car going over the side, and this totally took over my mind as I came closer to any bridge.

I would become almost paralyzed by fear, breaking out into a sweat, almost unable to breathe. I would call for Jesus to get me over, and He always did, but still the fear would come back the next time. So I would try and avoid using bridges, or I would just not go where I wanted to.

As a result, I was not enjoying my life to its fullest—as I was living in bondage.

One Sunday in church, a friend of mine came over with a book, plunked it into my lap, and told me to read it. The book was *The Bondage Breaker*. I read through it and went through the Steps to Freedom in Christ in the back.

When I first read it, I didn't sleep very well. That first night I dreamed that Satan was taking me from room to room in a large mansion and was showing me everything he said he owned and how he would make it mine. I woke a number of times and found myself repeating Scriptures out loud and calling on the Lord for help.

The second night, I didn't have the dreams, but I woke up about 3 A.M. shaking violently, as if terribly frightened. I felt no inner fear, only this physical manifestation. I fell back asleep and woke up again an hour-and-a-half later. As soon as I awoke, I felt very refreshed and calm, and I sensed the Lord saying to me, "I told you that I would never leave you nor forsake you."

Soon after that I had to cross a bridge. When I came to within 100 feet of it, I loudly said, "In the name of Jesus Christ, I bind you, spirit of fear. For Jesus is driving this car now, and I am only the passenger!" I sailed over that bridge.

I do not experience that fear any longer, and I know I no longer own it. And it certainly does not own me!

A Plan of Action

Let's summarize what you have done so far. You have submitted to God and resisted the devil. You have identified your fears and the lies behind them. You understand how those fears have kept you from living a responsible life or compelled you to compromise your witness for Christ. You are now halfway home because a problem well-stated is half-solved.

The next step is to face the fear and prayerfully work out a plan to overcome it. When Rich finally discovered the root of Brian's fear, he knew Brian had to face it. That's why they took him out for ice cream. Brian wasn't truly free until he took the first few bites. By his own admission, that's when he felt the fear snap in two inside of him.

The girl who told about her experience driving over bridges was exercising faith. By faith she verbally resisted the devil (as Jesus showed us to do when He was tempted in the wilderness), and she declared that Jesus was in charge. Then by faith she drove over the bridge. She broke the back of fear when she called on the name of the Lord and drove across.

Years ago I learned that one of my students hadn't spoken to her father in six months. The tension in the home was unbearable. I asked her if she would be willing to work out a plan of action to overcome her fear of him. Somehow she needed to break the ice. I asked her what she thought would happen if she just said, "Hi, Dad," when he came home that night. She wasn't sure, so we considered the possibilities. He could get mad, he could say "hi" back, or he could do nothing. It was the latter possibility that she feared the most.

Then we worked out a plan for each possible response by her father. Then I asked her to commit to saying "hi" that night. She agreed to do that and then call me afterwards. About 7:30 that evening I got a call from a joyful young lady who reported, "He said 'hi' back!"

Fear is like a mirage in the desert. It seems so real until you move toward it, then it disappears into thin air. But as long as we back away from fear, it will haunt us and grow in size till it's giant.

There's a Coast Guard story about an old sea captain who ordered his crew to sea in the midst of a raging storm. A young seaman cried out, "We can't go out—we'll never come back!" To this the captain replied, "We must go out—we don't have to come back!" Fear gets swallowed up when we decide to fulfill our responsibilities.

In Christ we have all been allotted a measure of faith. To exercise that faith we must have sound judgment. To accomplish the goal of complete freedom, we must take that first step in the right direction. If your plan to overcome fear includes confronting other people, it is helpful to determine in advance how you will respond to their positive or negative reactions. In other words, the plan shouldn't just include the first step—it should also include possible second and third steps.

Many learned fears should be overcome in bite-size steps. Making step-by-step progress toward a goal is the key. In the following example, as you'll see, each step is a slightly larger "bite-size" chunk than the one before.

Plan for Overcoming Fear of Elevators

1. Look at elevators, watching them come and go.
2. Stand in a stationary elevator with a trusted friend.
3. Stand in a stationary elevator alone.
4. Travel up or down one floor with your friend.
5. Travel up or down one floor alone, with your friend waiting outside the elevator on the floor where you will arrive.
6. Travel two or three floors with your friend.
7. Travel two or three floors alone, with your friend waiting outside the elevator on the floor where you will arrive.
8. Extend the number of floors you travel, first with your friend with you and then alone with your friend waiting outside the elevator.
9. Travel on an elevator alone without your friend being there.[2]

Depending on the severity of your fear, these steps could take place in one day or over a period of days, weeks, or even months. The main idea is to keep moving forward. If you find yourself beginning to walk in fear, exercise your authority in Christ over any attack of the enemy and make the choice to push through the fear and walk by faith in God.

Choose Faith, Not Fear

Most fears are struggles against our own flesh patterns developed in the past. But whenever you sense your fear or panic attack is from the enemy, make the following declaration of your authority over the devil:

> *In the name and authority of the Lord Jesus Christ, I bind all lying spirits causing fear and anxiety in me. I resist Satan and all his evil workers in the name of Jesus, and by His authority I command them to leave my presence. I declare that Satan is already defeated—by Jesus at the cross. God has not given me a spirit of fear, but of power, love, and a sound mind. I therefore reject all fear and choose to walk by faith in the Holy Spirit's power, live in the light of God's love, and think with the sound mind of Christ.*

May the Lord grant you the courage to confront your fears and to know the peace that David must have known when he wrote, "Even though I walk through the valley of the shadow of death, I fear no evil, for You are with me" (Psalm 23:4).

Stomping Out Fear

Read:
Psalm 34:4-7

Reflect:

What did you relate to most in Brian's personal ordeal of fear of sugar and cavities? What was the key lie that Brian was believing? What happened when he believed the truth and faced his fear?

Why is the first step to overcoming a fear getting radically right with God? Have you processed through the "Fear Finder"? If not, go through the "Fear Finder" section in this chapter now.

How did God use the "Fear Finder" to help you identify your fears? What lies did you identify that were behind your fears? How have your fears prevented you from doing what is right and responsible? Have your fears affected your witness for Christ?

What plans did you put in place to overcome your fear (like the elevator plan outlined in this chapter)?

Respond:

Dear heavenly Father, I want to thank You for showing me how awesome and mighty You are. When I focus on You I

*understand just how small, tiny, and insignificant my fears
are in comparison to who You are as God. I no longer want
to walk in bondage to my petty fears, so I choose to submit
to You each day and resist the devil so that my tiny fears will
vanish.*

*Today You have shown me the source of many of my fears.
I'm thankful that You're the source of all my strength and that
I will never lack strength if I continue to depend on You and
call upon Your name. So I call upon Your name, the name
of Jesus, and I call upon Your Spirit to fill me up to the full
with all Your strength and mighty power. In Jesus' name I
pray, amen.*

Building a Stronghold of Faith

Eight

A STRONGHOLD IS A WELL-DEFENDED PLACE. There are fleshly strongholds (see chapter 1), but there are godly strongholds as well. Apart from Christ, we develop our own means of coping with life and defending ourselves. Those fleshly strongholds of the mind are characterized by thoughts raised up against the knowledge of God, including doubt, unbelief, fear, and anxiety.

God, however, has given us superior weapons designed to break down fleshly strongholds such as controlling fears and anxieties. Rather than asking us to defend ourselves, however, *He* wants to become our defense and stronghold. David wrote, "The LORD is a refuge for the oppressed, a stronghold in times of trouble. Those who know your name will trust in you, for you, LORD, have never forsaken those who seek you" (Psalm 9:9-10 NIV).

God is faithful. He never allows His children to be tested beyond their ability to escape or endure (see 1 Corinthians 10:13). Regardless of the afflictions that we experience in this fallen world, we have the assurance that "the God of all grace, who called you to His eternal glory in Christ, will Himself perfect, confirm, strengthen and establish you" (1 Peter 5:10).

So why do people turn to the temporary things of this world to find peace and comfort? Some have little or no knowledge of God. Others, because of negative experiences with the church or with religious people, may have rejected God as being cold, harsh, or uncaring. Some people who have been abused or deeply hurt in the past have wondered, "Where was God when I needed Him?" But according to David, God is always there for us:

> O LORD, you have searched me and you know me. You know when I sit and when I rise; you perceive my thoughts from afar. You discern my going out and my lying down; you are familiar with all my ways. Before a word is on my tongue you know it completely, O LORD.
>
> You hem me in—behind and before; you have laid your hand upon me. Such knowledge is too wonderful for me, too lofty for me to attain.
>
> Where can I go from your Spirit? Where can I flee from your presence? If I go up to the heavens, you are there; if I make my bed in the depths, you are there. If I rise on the wings of the dawn, if I settle on the far side of the sea, even there your hand will guide me, your right hand will hold me fast.
>
> If I say, "Surely the darkness will hide me and the light become night around me," even the darkness will not be dark to you; the night will shine like the day, for darkness is as light to you (Psalm 139:1-12 NIV).

When we are rightly related to God, we will cry out from our hearts, "Abba! Father!" God longs for us to experience that kind of closeness to Him.

The True God

Check this out—it will help you renew your mind to the truth of who God really is. Verbally renounce the lies that you may have

The Truth About Our Heavenly Father

I renounce the lie that my Father God is...	*I joyfully accept the truth that my Father God is...*
1. distant and uninterested	1. intimate and involved (Psalm 139:1-8)
2. insensitive and uncaring	2. kind and compassionate (Psalm 103:8-14)
3. stern and demanding	3. accepting and filled with joy and love (Zephaniah 3:17; Romans 15:7)
4. passive and cold	4. warm and affectionate (Isaiah 40:11; Hosea 11:3-4)
5. absent or too busy for me	5. always with me and eager to be with me (Jeremiah 31:20; Ezekiel 34:11-16; Hebrews 13:5)
6. never satisfied with what I do; impatient, angry	6. patient and slow to anger (Exodus 34:6; 2 Peter 3:9)
7. mean, cruel, or abusive	7. loving, gentle, and protective of me (Psalm 18:2; Jeremiah 31:3; Isaiah 42:3)
8. trying to take all the fun out of life	8. trustworthy and wants to give me a full life; His will is good, perfect, and acceptable (Lamentations 3:22-23; John 10:10; Romans 12:1-2)
9. controlling or manipulative	9. full of grace and mercy; He gives me freedom to fail (Luke 15:11-16; Hebrews 4:15-16)
10. condemning or unforgiving	10. tenderhearted and forgiving; His heart and arms are always open to me (Psalm 130:1-4; Luke 15:17-24)
11. nit-picking, exacting, or perfectionistic	11. committed to my growth and proud of me as His growing child (Romans 8:28-29; 2 Corinthians 7:4; Hebrews 12:5-11)

I am the apple of His eye!
(Deuteronomy 32:10 NIV)

believed about your heavenly Father, and announce the truths about Him from the Word of God. Work your way down the lists, one by one, left to right. Begin each one with the statement in bold print at the top of that list.

Once we have broken the back of unbelief and fear in our lives, we are free to rebuild a stronghold of faith. We keep fear from returning by worshiping God in spirit and truth (see John 4:23-24). We worship Him in spirit when we are born again and filled with His Holy Spirit. We worship Him in truth by calling upon His name and rightly ascribing to Him His divine attributes.

The Names of God

The more we get to know God, the more we discover His protective care. "The name of the LORD is a strong tower; the righteous runs into it and is safe"(Proverbs 18:10). God's names are descriptive of who He is; they also reveal His character. Every fear we experience ultimately has its antidote in knowing and trusting in God's name. God says "fear not" because He is always with us to protect and guide us:

> Be strong and courageous. Do not be afraid or terrified because of them, for the LORD your God goes with you; he will never leave you nor forsake you (Deuteronomy 31:6 NIV).

> David also said to Solomon his son, "Be strong and courageous, and do the work. Do not be afraid or discouraged, for the LORD God, my God, is with you" (1 Chronicles 28:20 NIV).

> The LORD is with me; I will not be afraid. What can man do to me? (Psalm 118:6 NIV).

> I am the LORD, your God, who takes hold of your right hand and says to you, "Do not fear; I will help you" (Isaiah 41:13 NIV).

God with Us

Time and time again God promises to be with us. In fact, one of the names given to the Messiah is "Immanuel," as prophesied in Isaiah 7:14 and fulfilled in Matthew 1:23: "'The virgin shall be with child and shall bear a Son, and they shall call His name Immanuel,' which translated means, 'God with us.'" Jesus is Immanuel, God with us. When He walked on earth, He was God with us in the flesh. Then Jesus sent the Holy Spirit, "another Helper," one who is just like Christ Himself, to be with us (see John 14:16).

Imagine yourself in a very stressful and frightening situation. Now picture the Lord Jesus visibly present with you as you go through that situation. What happened? Were you more confident in your heart as you thought about your Lord being there with you? The Lord says, "I will dwell in them and walk among them; and I will be their God, and they shall be My people" (2 Corinthians 6:16).

It would probably be easier to be courageous if Jesus were visibly present with us, but He's not. That is another reason why we need to worship Him—so that we are reminded of His invisible presence. "We walk by faith, not by sight," and "faith is the assurance of things hoped for, the conviction of things not seen" (2 Corinthians 5:7; Hebrews 11:1).

Actually, we are better off without Jesus being physically present. In Jesus' own words, "I tell you the truth, it is to your advantage that I go away; for if I do not go away, the Helper will not come to you; but if I go, I will send Him to you" (John 16:7). It is better to have the indwelling presence of the Holy Spirit than the physical presence of Jesus. If Jesus were physically present by our side, the best we could do would be to imitate Him, and He would not be omnipresent. But with the Spirit living inside of us, we can actually become like Jesus, and He is always and everywhere present with us!

Faith Versus Fear

Peter demonstrated the contrast between faith and fear in Matthew 14. A person was walking on the water toward the disciples' boat. Once the disciples realized that it was Jesus, not a ghost, Peter called out, "Lord, if it is You, command me to come to You on the water" (verse 28). Jesus said to him, "Come!"

Peter stepped out of the boat and was miraculously walking on the water, approaching Jesus. Steadfast of heart and seeing with eyes of faith, he continued to walk toward Jesus. Suddenly he was distracted: "But seeing the wind, he became frightened, and beginning to sink, he cried out, 'Lord, save me!'" (verse 30).

Jesus took hold of his hand and brought Peter safely back to the boat. But there is no mistaking the disappointment in Jesus' words: "You of little faith, why did you doubt?" (verse 31). As if to drive home His point, the wind stopped immediately upon Jesus' entry into the boat. Truly there is no real reason to fear when Jesus is present.

It is our conviction that every anxiety disorder can ultimately be dissolved by the knowledge and presence of God. That is why the exhortation of Scripture is to "seek the Lord" and "fix your eyes on Jesus" (see Isaiah 55:6; Jeremiah 29:13; Amos 5:4; Hebrews 12:2). We will experience His peace when we keep our eyes of faith trained on Him, walking intimately with Him.

Know God's Name

When Melchizedek—the king and priest—blessed Abram, he said, "Blessed be Abram of God Most High, possessor of heaven and earth" (Genesis 14:19). He called God by His name *El Elyon*, which means "the God who is Creator of all things and who is above all other gods." Why should we yield to fear when we can trust in the God who is greater than all things, including fear?

When Moses, the deliverer, was preparing to confront Pharaoh and lead the Israelites from Egypt, God revealed His name to him: "I AM WHO I AM" (Exodus 3:14). He is the eternal, self-existent, covenant-keeping God. Why should we fear the future when God is eternal and knows the end from the beginning (Isaiah 46:10)? He is the Alpha and the Omega, the first and the last, the beginning and the end, the One who is and who was and who is to come (Revelation 1:8; 22:13).

When the prophet Isaiah spoke of the coming birth of the Messiah, he said, "His name will be called Wonderful Counselor, Mighty God, Eternal Father, Prince of Peace" (Isaiah 9:6). Why should we be anxious about the decisions we need to make when He is our Wonderful Counselor? Why should we be afraid to step out in faith when our Mighty God is there to provide us with strength? Why should we feel anxious and insecure when our Eternal Father dwells within us? And why let fear and anxiety overwhelm us when the Prince of Peace will never leave us?

Prayerfully meditate on the following names of God. Ask the Lord to show you which of them is the "strong tower" you need today to combat fear and anxiety in your life.

The Fear-Busting Names of God

Jehovah-jireh . . . . The Lord will provide (Genesis 22:14)

El Shaddai . . . . The One is mighty to shed forth and pour out sustenance and blessing (Genesis 17:1-2)

Jehovah-sabaoth . . . . . The Lord of the hosts of heaven (Psalm 24:10)

Jehovah-rophe . . . . The Lord our healer (Exodus 15:26)

Jehovah-shalom . . . . . . The Lord is peace (Judges 6:24)

Jehovah-rohi . . . . The Lord our Shepherd (Psalm 23:1)

Jehovah-shammah. . . . The Lord is there (Ezekiel 48:35)

Jehovah-nissi . . . . The Lord is my banner (Exodus 17:15)

Jehovah-tsidkenu. . . . . The Lord our righteousness (Jeremiah 23:5-6)

Studying these names of God may be one of the best faith-building exercises you can do. Romans 12:2 teaches us that we are transformed through the renewing of our minds. In other words, our lives are changed as our minds are changed by the truth.

The name "Jesus" itself is full of grace, truth, and power. His name means "salvation." "God highly exalted Him, and bestowed on Him the name which is above every name, so that at the name of Jesus *every knee will bow*, of those who are in heaven and on earth and under the earth" (Philippians 2:9-10, emphasis added). We encourage you to make it a regular practice to worship the Lord Jesus by using His names. In the process you will find your faith growing and your fear fleeing. We have listed some of these glorious names to help you get started.

The Awesome Names of Jesus

- Advocate (1 John 2:1)
- Alpha and Omega (Revelation 21:6)
- Anointed One (Psalm 2:2)
- Author and perfecter of faith (Hebrews 12:2)
- Beginning and end (Revelation 21:6)
- Beloved (Ephesians 1:6)
- Bread of Life (John 6:35)
- Bright morning star (Revelation 22:16)

- Chief corner stone (Mark 12:10)
- Chief shepherd (1 Peter 5:4)
- Christ (Matthew 16:16-17)
- Counselor (Isaiah 9:6)
- Deliverer (Romans 11:26)
- Eternal Father (Isaiah 9:6)
- Faithful and True (Revelation 19:11)
- First and last (Revelation 22:13)
- God (John 1:1,14)
- Good Shepherd (John 10:11)
- Guardian of souls (1 Peter 2:25)
- Head of the church (Colossians 1:18)
- Heir of all things (Hebrews 1:2)
- High Priest (Hebrews 4:14)
- Holy One (1 John 2:20)
- Horn of salvation (Luke 1:69)
- I Am (John 8:58)
- Immanuel (Matthew 1:23)
- King of Israel (John 12:13)
- King of kings (Revelation 17:14)
- Lamb (Revelation 13:8)
- Life (John 14:6)
- Light of the world (John 8:12)
- Lion of Judah (Revelation 5:5)
- Living stone (1 Peter 2:4)
- Lord (John 21:7)
- Lord Jesus Christ (1 Peter 1:3)
- Lord of lords (Revelation 17:14)
- Messiah (John 4:25-26)

- Mighty God (Isaiah 9:6)
- Our Passover lamb (1 Corinthians 5:7)
- Prince of Peace (Isaiah 9:6)
- Prophet (Deuteronomy 18:15,18)
- Redeemer (Isaiah 59:20)
- Resurrection and life (John 11:25)
- Righteous One (Isaiah 53:11)
- Rock (1 Corinthians 10:4)
- Savior (Luke 2:11)
- Son of God (Romans 1:4)
- Teacher (John 13:13)
- True Vine (John 15:1)
- Truth (John 14:6)
- Wonderful (Isaiah 9:6)
- Word of God (Revelation 19:13)

The Holy Spirit

Knowing the true nature of God the Holy Spirit is faith-building as well. He is called

- Spirit of truth (John 16:13)
- Spirit of life (Romans 8:2)
- Spirit of adoption (Romans 8:15)
- Spirit of the living God (2 Corinthians 3:3)
- Holy Spirit of promise (Ephesians 1:13)
- Spirit of grace (Hebrews 10:29)
- Spirit of Christ (1 Peter 1:11)
- Spirit of glory (1 Peter 4:14).

As we are filled with the Holy Spirit, we are given a heart of praise, thanksgiving, and humility (Ephesians 5:18-21) and the power to be Christ's witnesses (Acts 1:8). We can walk by the Spirit's power and not give in to fleshly desires (Galatians 5:16-18). We are also gifted for His service and brought into unity with other believers in Christ (1 Corinthians 12). And we can overcome fear with the power, love, and sound mind He gives us (see 2 Timothy 1:7).

Renewing Our Minds

How do words of Scripture renew our minds and transform our lives? The non-Christian cannot perceive the truth, but we have the mind of Christ (1 Corinthians 2:14-16). On the other hand, the Spirit of God will not do our thinking for us. We must choose to believe the truth and let the Word of Christ richly dwell within us (Colossians 3:16). One effective way to do this is by meditating upon the Word of God. Meditation is a biblical practice—check out these verses:

> How blessed is the man who does not walk in the counsel of the wicked, nor stand in the path of sinners, nor sit in the seat of scoffers! But his delight is in the law of the LORD, and in His law he meditates day and night. He will be like a tree firmly planted by streams of water, which yields its fruit in its season and its leaf does not wither; and in whatever he does, he prospers (Psalm 1:1-3).

> This book of the law shall not depart from your mouth, but you shall meditate on it day and night, so that you may be careful to do according to all that is written in it; for then you will make your way prosperous, and then you will have success (Joshua 1:8).

The main difference between ungodly meditation and biblical meditation is the object of the meditation. The blessed man's "delight is in the law of the LORD, and in His law he meditates day and night" (Psalm 1:2). After Paul tells the believers in Philippi to pray instead of worrying, he adds these powerful words:

> Finally, brethren, whatever is true, whatever is honorable, whatever is right, whatever is pure, whatever is lovely, whatever is of good repute, if there is any excellence and if anything worthy of praise, dwell on these things. The things you have learned and received and heard and seen in me, practice these things; and the God of peace shall be with you (Philippians 4:8-9).

What a promise! Prayerful meditation followed by obedience connects us with the peace of God and the God of peace (Philippians 4:6-9). It's hard to imagine a more encouraging word to someone who has been struggling with fear and anxiety. Therefore, it is critical that we approach the Word of God as the life-giving food it is, chewing on it day and night. In prayer, we ask the Lord what it means and how we can apply God's Word to our lives. The more we meditate on the riches of its wisdom and obey what it says, the more it becomes a secure belt of truth around us and a flashing sword in our hand (see Ephesians 6:14,17). The more our faith grows, the more fear flees.

Our Identity in Christ

Knowing God is the most important part of our belief system. Knowing who we are in Christ and how He perceives us is the second most important part of our belief system. How does God view His people? First of all, we are His children (John 1:12), chosen by Him, holy and dearly loved (Colossians 3:12). We have been raised up and seated with Christ so that in the ages to come, God can show us the surpassing riches of grace in kindness toward us (Ephesians 2:6-7).

A story is told about the great painter Leonardo da Vinci. Upon the completion of one of his greatest works, the Mona Lisa, the people who saw the painting immediately declared it to be a masterpiece. They claimed that this portrait was the most beautiful picture of a woman ever painted by anyone.

One day several men gathered at a local tavern, and they began to boast about Leonardo's incredible talent. They boasted that he could no doubt make *anyone* look more handsome or beautiful if he wanted to. All the painter would need to do would be to embellish the canvas with his special skills—and even an ordinary person could be transformed by his keen eye and skillful painting.

Soon a challenge came out of the crowd. A man stepped forward and said, "Leonardo, can you make this man beautiful?" and with that he pointed to an extremely ugly and homely old man who had been disfigured by long, hard years of life and toil. Embarrassed, the old man tried to wave away all the attention. But Leonardo stood up and declared, "I will paint this man."

Several days later, everyone in the area began gathering together, curious to see if in fact the great da Vinci could transform this ugly old man into something of beauty. The veiled painting was set up in the tavern, and everyone waited with great anticipation for Leonardo to unveil his painting.

As the veil was lifted, everyone gasped in horror! The painting was not beautiful—rather it was an exact depiction of the old man.

"What is this!" one man yelled from the crowd. "You have failed—why, he isn't beautiful at all."

"Oh, no," Leonardo protested. "He is beautiful, for everything that God creates is beautiful—and who am I to alter God's perfection."

We have all been created by the mighty hand of God—each of us is His masterpiece. What Christ has done for us can't be added to. We are complete in Him.

Knowing the love of God and who we are in Christ affects how we live our lives, as 1 John 3:1-3 reveals:

> See how great a love the Father has bestowed upon us, that we would be called children of God; and such we are. For this reason the world does not know us, because it did not know Him. Beloved, now we are children of God, and it has not appeared as yet what we will be. We know that when He appears, we will be like Him, because we will see Him just as He is. And everyone who has this hope fixed on Him purifies himself, just as He is pure.

Jesus gave Himself up for us, shedding His blood and dying on the cross, and the Bible tells us that there is no greater love possible than laying down your life for a friend (John 15:13). Jesus has already demonstrated His love for us in a way that cannot be surpassed. And yet His love for the church did not end with that one incredible sacrifice on the cross. He continually "nourishes and cherishes" the church, of which every believer is a part (see Ephesians 5:29).

The Lord Jesus has sealed us with the Holy Spirit of promise, who is the "down payment" of what is going to come (Ephesians 1:13-14). The Spirit will remain with us and in us until the time we are safely brought into Jesus' presence.

In addition to declaring that we are God's children, the Bible speaks of us in other ways that show God's deep concern and loving protection over us. We are Jesus' sheep, and He is the Good Shepherd (John 10). We are the body of Christ, and Jesus is the head (1 Corinthians 12:12-28; Colossians 1:18). We are a royal priesthood, and Jesus is the high priest (1 Peter 2:9; Hebrews 7:26-27). We are a holy nation, and He is the ruler of it (1 Peter 2:9; Isaiah 9:6-7). We are saints, and He is the One who has made us holy (1 Corinthians 1:2; Hebrews 10:10).

Forgiven. Cleansed. Given eternal life. New creations in Christ. Indwelt by the Holy Spirit. Redeemed. Chosen. Declared not guilty. Given the very righteousness of Christ. Gifted by the Spirit. Called into kingdom service. All these things and much, much more God has done for us because of His amazing grace.

The cross was where the work was finished, dealing a death blow to sin and death. The empty tomb was where the work was done that assures us of eternal life. In the presence of Jesus in heaven is where the work will be glorified, consummating our marriage to the Lamb for eternity. Has not God truly demonstrated beyond a shadow of a doubt the extent of His love for His people? Can we not, in light of all this, give ourselves unreservedly into His hands and trust Him to provide for and protect us? In light of this, Paul said,

> I urge you, brethren, by the mercies of God, to present your bodies a living and holy sacrifice, acceptable to God, which is your spiritual service of worship. And do not be conformed to this world, but be transformed by the renewing of your mind, so that you may prove what the will of God is, that which is good and acceptable and perfect (Romans 12:1-2).

Stomping Out Fear

Read:
1 John 3:1-3

Reflect:
Satan's strategy is to "divide and conquer," so he tries to isolate us and cut us off from the encouraging fellowship of other believers. God never intended or expected us to live the Christian life alone. Make the choice today to become involved in Christian fellowship if you are not already doing so.

The need for fellowship with other believers will become more and more critical as time goes on (Hebrews 10:25). We need to know that we are not alone in our fight against fear. God has created us with a need for Him and one another, and we will be more safe and secure within the context of close human relationships. Use the following list—"Who Are We?"—and the group resolution following to strengthen your corporate identity and ties with other believers.

Who Are We?

- We are brothers and sisters in Christ (1 John 3:14)
- We are growing into a holy temple in the Lord (Ephesians 2:19-21)
- We are being built together into a dwelling of God in the Spirit (Ephesians 2:22)

- We are a chosen race (1 Peter 2:9)
- We are a royal priesthood (1 Peter 2:9)
- We are a holy nation (1 Peter 2:9)
- We are a people for God's own possession, called out of darkness into His marvelous light, called to proclaim His excellencies (1 Peter 2:9-10)
- We once were not a people, but now we are the people of God (1 Peter 2:10)
- We once had not received mercy, but now we have received mercy (1 Peter 2:10)
- We are the body of Christ, and individual members of it (1 Corinthians 12:27)
- We all suffer when one of our members suffers (1 Corinthians 12:26)
- We all rejoice when one of our members rejoices (1 Corinthians 12:26)
- We need each other (1 Corinthians 12:14-27)
- We have different gifts, but the same Spirit (1 Corinthians 12:4)
- We have different ministries, but the same Lord (1 Corinthians 12:5)
- We have different results, but the same God who is working in all things (1 Corinthians 12:6)
- We are already one in the Spirit in the bond of peace (Ephesians 4:3)
- We are the bride of the Lamb, Jesus Christ (Revelation 21:2,9)

Respond:

Dear heavenly Father, I renounce any spirit of isolation, division, or competition. I rejoice that we are one body in Christ—having one Spirit, one hope of our calling, one Lord, one faith, one baptism, and one God, the Father, who is over all and through all and in all.

Therefore, I resolve by God's grace to consider how to stimulate others to love and good deeds, encouraging them day after day. I resolve to accept others in Christ, just as I have been accepted by God in Christ. I resolve by the power of the Holy Spirit to exercise the spiritual gifts given to me, speaking the truth in love so that I can grow up in all aspects into Him, who is the head, even Christ.

In so doing, I know that the whole body, being fitted and held together by that which every joint supplies, according to the proper working of each individual part, causes the growth of the body for the building up of itself in love. In Jesus' name I pray, amen.

(See Ephesians 4:1-16; Hebrews 10:24-25; Romans 15:7.)

The Fear that Destroys All Other Fears

Nine

WHEN WAS THE LAST TIME YOU HEARD a youth pastor give a message on the "fear of the Lord" or read a book on the subject? Maybe it's been a long time. Maybe this is the first time. But the fear of the Lord isn't an outdated concept belonging in the dusty archives of hellfire-and-brimstone preachers: "The fear of the LORD is clean, enduring forever" (Psalm 19:9). This important theme occurs consistently throughout the Bible, from Genesis 20:11 to Revelation 19:5.

Fearing God is not a law-based principle. Rather, it is an eternally enduring aspect of our relationship to God. Isaiah foretold that the fear of God would rest on Jesus the Messiah, and He was the One in whom grace and truth were realized (John 1:17).

What does it mean to "fear the Lord"? Does it mean that we are supposed to be afraid of God? Doesn't perfect love cast out fear (see 1 John 4:18)? How can we love God and fear Him at the same time? And how does the fear of God destroy all unhealthy fears?

Defining the Fear of God

The following verses from the psalms will help us figure out what it means to fear the Lord:

161

> You who fear the LORD, praise Him; all you descendants of Jacob, glorify Him, and stand in awe of Him, all you descendants of Israel (Psalm 22:23).

> Let all the earth fear the LORD; let all the inhabitants of the world stand in awe of Him (Psalm 33:8).

> My flesh trembles in fear of you; I stand in awe of your laws (Psalm 119:120 NIV).

To fear God is to be awestruck with God's character and Word. It is a state of deep reverence that can cause us to tremble before Him because of His righteous judgments. The fear of the Lord is also joyful praise and worship of His glory, resulting in humble obedience to His will. "Holy fear…is God-given, enabling men to reverence God's authority, obey His commandments, and hate and shun all form of evil." [1]

John gives us a vivid picture of what it means to fear the Lord. He was "in the Spirit on the Lord's day" when he heard a voice behind him like a loud trumpet (Revelation 1:9-10). When he turned around, he saw a vision of the reigning Christ that overwhelmed him:

> Having turned I saw seven golden lampstands; and in the middle of the lampstands I saw one like a son of man, clothed in a robe reaching to the feet, and girded across His chest with a golden sash. And His head and His hair were white like white wool, like snow; and His eyes were like a flame of fire. His feet were like burnished bronze, when it has been made to glow in a furnace, and His voice was like the sound of many waters. In His right hand He held seven stars, and out of His mouth came a sharp two-edged sword; and His face was like the sun shining in its strength. When I saw

> Him, I fell at His feet like a dead man (Revelation 1:12-
> 17).

John knew and loved Jesus with all his heart. He had spent three years with Him, witnessing His miracles and His loving, gracious heart. But he had never seen the Lord Jesus like this. All John's strength was drained from his body as he collapsed in holy fear. He needed a touch and a word from Jesus Himself in order to be revived. "He placed His right hand on me, saying, 'Do not be afraid; I am the first and the last, and the living One; and I was dead, and behold, I am alive forevermore, and I have the keys of death and of Hades'" (Revelation 1:17-18).

John needed to see Jesus in a new light, and so do we. He had known Jesus as the miracle-working Messiah who displayed His tender mercies. But now John saw Him as the Creator God, Judge of the earth, and Head of the church. In the mind of John, the gentle Jesus suddenly became the great "I AM."

It is hard for us to grasp the greatness of God. Many people prefer to think of Him as a kindly old grandfather who winks at sin and dutifully hands out treats whenever they ask for them. Such a distorted concept of God will cause no one to fear Him. Job's friend Elihu, however, painted a picture of God that should help us learn to fear Him:

> As we cannot look at the sun for its brightness when the winds have cleared away the clouds, neither can we gaze at the terrible majesty of God breaking forth upon us from heaven, clothed in dazzling splendor. We cannot imagine the power of the Almighty, and yet he is so just and merciful that he does not destroy us. No wonder men everywhere fear him! (Job 37:21-24 TLB).

Psalm 33 teaches that God spoke—and propelled billions of galaxies into existence. They remain in place by the word of His power (Hebrews 1:3). Mighty leaders and nations make their plans, and God effortlessly thwarts them, revealing to the world that He is the ruler over the realm of mankind (Daniel 4:17). Nations that vie for world power and domination are as a speck of dust or drop of water to Him (Isaiah 40:15).

Fear Versus Being Afraid

God is far superior to all other fear objects, but He is also kind and good. He is to be feared, but God does not want us to be afraid of Him. When Jesus touched John, He said, "Do not be afraid" (Revelation 1:17). God is our "Abba, Father" (Galatians 4:6). He delights in His children, quieting us in His love and rejoicing over us with shouts of joy (Zephaniah 3:17). It would grieve the heart of our heavenly Father if we were to fearfully run away from Him or slink away in suspicion and mistrust. Even when we sin, His love for us does not change. The Bible says that the kindness of God led you to turn away from your sin (see Romans 2:4).

We Should Not Fear God's Purifying of Our Lives

God is a forgiving God, and He is also a purifying God. He will do a deeper work in our lives beyond salvation. He will take us far beyond simple survival to real *revival*. This purifying process may be painful at times, but it is always for our good. God is in the process of conforming us to His image. His ultimate concern is to purify the church.

We should not be afraid of this purifying work of God. We should be thankful because He is stripping away our self-sufficiency in order for us to be fully clothed in Christ. We will only be secure in the unshakable kingdom of Jesus.

It's kind of like the wood sculptor who was asked how he was able to carve such beautiful birds. Picking up one of his master-pieces, the sculptor smiled and replied, "It's simple. I just cut away everything that doesn't look like the bird." God is cutting away everything in us that doesn't look like Jesus.

The Judgment Seat of Christ

Every believer will someday appear before the judgment seat of Christ. This is not a judgment for sins, for we have already been forgiven of all our sins and made alive together with Christ. Jesus "canceled out the certificate of debt consisting of decrees against us, which was hostile to us; and He has taken it out of the way, having nailed it to the cross" (Colossians 2:14). "There is now no condemnation for those who are in Christ Jesus" (Romans 8:1). The believer's final judgment is for works in order to receive rewards, as 1 Corinthians 3:11-15 teaches:

> No man can lay a foundation other than the one which is laid, which is Jesus Christ. Now if any man builds upon the foundation with gold, silver, precious stones, wood, hay, straw, each man's work will become evident; for the day will show it because it is to be revealed with fire, and the fire itself will test the quality of each man's work. If any man's work which he has built upon it remains, he will receive a reward. If any man's work is burned up, he shall suffer loss; but he himself will be saved, yet so as through fire.

For believers in Christ, where we spend eternity has already been decided, but how we spend eternity is still to be judged according to our faithfulness. We have only one life and it will soon be past—only what's done for Christ will last. Whatever we have done in the flesh will not last. Work done for our own glory, in our own strength, will be burned up. That which we have done for the glory of God is like gold, silver, and precious jewels. It will stand the test of fire, and we will be rewarded. Knowing that we will be held accountable before God is a powerful motivating force.

How we live life on earth will determine our rewards in heaven. Peter's words are good counsel for daily living in light of eternity:

> Prepare your minds for action, keep sober in spirit, fix your hope completely on the grace to be brought to you at the revelation of Jesus Christ. As obedient children, do not be conformed to the former lusts which were yours in your ignorance, but like the Holy One who called you, be holy yourselves also in all your behavior; because it is written, "You shall be holy, for I am holy."
>
> If you address as Father the One who impartially judges according to each one's work, conduct yourselves in fear during the time of your stay on earth (1 Peter 1:13-17).

We long to see Jesus face to face and hear Him say, "Well done, good and faithful servant! You have been faithful with a few things; I will put you in charge of many things. Come and share your master's happiness!" (Matthew 25:21 NIV). As a child, I didn't fear the rod of discipline from my father. I feared the accountability. It was an issue of regret, not guilt. In a similar fashion, I don't want to stand before God someday and regret the way I lived my life as a believer. Whether in loss or in reward, we have the confidence that He loves us and will remember our sins no more.

Loving and Fearing God

God's love for us and our love for Him do not shut down the fear of God. Perfect love casts out the *fear of punishment* for our sins. Too many young Christians live in fear of punishment—they live as though the hammer of God will fall upon them if they make even the slightest mistake.

The hammer fell! It fell on Christ. The punishment we deserved has already fallen on Christ. That is the good news.

Loving God and fearing God are not mutually exclusive. Both are needed for a healthy spiritual life. They reflect the justice and mercy of God, which are opposite sides of the same coin. If we loved God without fearing Him, we could easily slip into laziness or license. If we feared God without loving Him we could easily become legalistic. The following Scriptures provide the biblical balance for both fearing and loving God:

> As high as the heavens are above the earth, so great is His lovingkindness toward those who fear Him.…Just as a father has compassion on his children, so the LORD has compassion on those who fear Him (Psalm 103:11,13).

> Let those who fear the LORD say: "His love endures forever" (Psalm 118:4 NIV).

> The LORD delights in those who fear him, who put their hope in his unfailing love (Psalm 147:11 NIV).

A Healthy Reverence

Let's illustrate how we can both love and fear our heavenly Father at the same time. Many of us have been blessed with fathers, mothers, aunts, uncles, grandparents, pastors, teachers, or coaches who have loved us dearly and believed in us deeply. Possibly they would have even given their lives for ours had they been faced with that decision.

As we reflect on those relationships, we see that we also had a great respect for those people. Their characters were reflections of the kinds of qualities we admired. Consequently, we had a strong motivation to please them. To do something that was dishonoring to them or that abused their trust was unthinkable. There was a very real sense in which we feared them.

Like most sons, I admired my father greatly growing up. He was tall and strong, kind and giving, involved with my life but not controlling. But I also knew that if I gave my mom any problems, I'd have to answer to my father and face his strong, firm, and loving hand of discipline. Here's a story that illustrates our relationship.

During my preteen years I went through different phases where I wanted to own exotic or unrealistic pets. Since we lived on a quarter-acre lot in suburban Philadelphia, our options were limited. Whatever I saw on TV, I wanted. One day it was a raccoon, the next it was a fox, then it was a dolphin, and so on. At one point I was sold on getting a horse. I had no idea how much a horse cost, though I knew it was more than I had. So I concocted a plan to give the "horse fund" a running start.

My father was paid on Thursday nights. After cashing his check, he would turn the money over to my mother, the family accountant. One evening my parents were watching TV in the living room. My father had just turned over his pay, in $20 bills, to my mother, and those bills were inside her purse by the phone in the hall. No one was around.

Quietly, I pulled one of those twenties out of the purse and took it to my room. After school the next day, I found a white envelope, put the money in it, stuffed it in my pocket, and took it down to the woods where I often played. Once I got there, I dragged the envelope around in the dirt to make it look like it had been there for some time.

Running home about an hour later, I burst in the door and announced the treasure that I had "found."

My mother was excited for me, encouraging me to use that money toward my horse.

So far, so good. The crime of the century had been pulled off, and no one was even suspicious. I never counted on my conscience betraying me, however. Hour by hour, I felt worse and worse. Finally, after baseball practice on Saturday afternoon, I couldn't stand it any more.

My father was sitting on a little hill waiting for me to finish. The closer I got to him, the worse I felt. How could I have stolen from my own parents? How could I have betrayed their trust and taken advantage of them like that? I was miserable. I didn't want to face them because I felt such shame, but I knew I could never be happy unless I told the truth.

When I reached my father, I burst into tears and confessed the whole crime. He put his arms around me and hugged me. I can still remember the sweetness of being accepted despite my stealing and lying.

After hugging me, my father floored me when he looked me in the eye and said, "Son, your mother and I knew you had stolen the money you said you'd found."

"You did?" My eyes bulged with the shock. I thought they'd suspected nothing.

He nodded sadly. "Yes, son, we knew. We were just waiting for you to come and tell us."

That did it. The floodgates of tears blew wide open. I had sinned. I had been discovered. But I had been loved anyway. And you'd better believe I never stole a thing from them again.

Benefits of Fearing God

The Bible promises that the fear of God will bring treasure of great blessing to our lives. Consider the following benefits to the one who fears God:

- *Guidance in life:* "Who is the man who fears the LORD? He will instruct him in the way he should choose" (Psalm 25:12).

- *Intimacy with God:* "The secret of the LORD is for those who fear Him, and He will make them know His covenant" (Psalm 25:14).

- *Preservation in testing:* "Behold, the eye of the LORD is on those who fear Him, on those who hope for His lovingkindness, to deliver their soul from death and to keep them alive in famine" (Psalm 33:18-19).

- *Provisions for life:* "O fear the LORD, you His saints; for to those who fear Him there is no want. The young lions do lack and suffer hunger; but they who seek the LORD shall not be in want of any good thing" (Psalm 34:9-10).

- *God's love:* "As high as the heavens are above the earth, so great is His lovingkindness toward those who fear Him" (Psalm 103:11).

- *God's compassion:* "Just as a father has compassion on his children, so the LORD has compassion on those who fear Him" (Psalm 103:13).

- *Physical health:* "Do not be wise in your own eyes; fear the LORD and turn away from evil. It will be healing to your body and refreshment to your bones" (Proverbs 3:7-8).

- *Wisdom and knowledge:* "The fear of the LORD is the beginning of wisdom, and the knowledge of the Holy One is understanding" (Proverbs 9:10).

- *Life and peace:* "The fear of the LORD leads to life, so that one may sleep satisfied, untouched by evil" (Proverbs 19:23).

- *Prosperity:* "The reward of humility and the fear of the LORD are riches, honor and life" (Proverbs 22:4).

The Bible is full of promises from God for the person who fears the Lord. Every one of them provides an antidote for the poison of controlling fears and anxieties. "As many as are the promises of God, in Him [Christ Jesus] they are yes; therefore also through Him is our Amen to the glory of God through us" (2 Corinthians 1:20). God's promises are true for all who are "in Christ." As believers, we simply respond to God in faith, saying "amen" to the blessings that are already ours—blessings that will last throughout our life's journey and on into eternity.

Going Home

At the turn of the century, a couple left their home in America in order to bring the gospel to Africa. For 50 years they labored on the mission field. In the process, they overcame their doubts and fears. God proved Himself faithful time and time again.

Now it was time to go back to the United States. Their physical strength and resources were nearly depleted. After saying farewell to their beloved Africa and all their lifelong friends, they boarded a ship to England. From there they sailed to New York on one of the queen's ships. It just so happened that the Queen of England was also on board.

As they pulled into New York harbor, the ship was greeted by tugboats saluting the arrival of the queen with their water cannons. As they gently docked at the pier, the United States Marine Band was there to greet them. All the passengers were given paper streamers to throw off the side of the ship in honor of the queen. A red carpet was rolled up the walkway to the ship. The rest of the passengers waited while the queen and all her entourage departed.

The band put their instruments away and the red carpet was rolled up. The first class passengers were next to disembark, and then the second, and finally the third class. While waiting their turn at the railing, this veteran missionary turned to his wife in a moment of sadness and said, "Look, honey—there's no one here to greet us. No one to welcome us home!"

She looked at her beloved husband of 50 years and said, "Honey, we're not home yet!"

> You, be sober in all things, endure hardship, do the work of an evangelist, fulfill your ministry.
>
> For I am already being poured out as a drink offering, and the time of my departure has come. I have fought the good fight, I have finished the course, I have kept the faith; in the future there is laid up for me the crown of righteousness, which the Lord, the righteous Judge, will award to me on that day; and not only to me, but also to all who have loved His appearing (2 Timothy 4:5-8).

This world is not your home.

Stomping Out Fear

Read:
Psalm 33:8-11

Reflect:
When was the last time you heard a youth pastor give a message on the "fear of the Lord" or read a book on the subject? Why do you think so few people nowadays study the fear of the Lord? Why is it important to have a proper understanding of the fear of the Lord?

What is the fear of the Lord? How would you define it? How do the love of God and the fear of the Lord work together? If we as Christians don't have a proper fear of the Lord, what might the consequences be? What happens if we carry it too far and forget the love of God?

How does the fear of the Lord help us personally—what are the benefits of fearing God? How does the fear of the Lord help us to destroy all other inappropriate fears in our lives?

Respond:

Dear heavenly Father, Your Word tells us that all the earth should fear the LORD; that all the inhabitants of the world should stand in awe of Him. Lord, I confess at times I have not held You in the highest awe and place of holiness as I should. I have not feared You in the right ways. I confess that I have sometimes let the world, the flesh, and the devil shape my view of You.

I reject what they have taught me about You, and I choose now to turn to You and Your Word. Thank You, Lord, that I can come before You and know that I will not be punished or sent away. Thank You that Your arms are always open to me because Christ was punished for my sin. I want to honor and revere You as my holy, loving God. In Jesus' name I pray, amen.

(See Psalm 33:8; Romans 8:1.)

Steps to Freedom in Christ

IT IS OUR DEEP BELIEF THAT the finished work of Jesus Christ and the presence of God in our lives are the only means by which we can solve personal and spiritual problems. Christ in us is our only hope (Colossians 1:27), and He alone can meet our deepest needs in life—acceptance, identity, security, and significance. These steps are not based on just another counseling technique. They are an encounter with God. He is the Wonderful Counselor. He is the One who helps us see our sin, confess it, and turn our back on it. He grants the repentance that leads to a knowledge of the truth that sets us free (2 Timothy 2:24-26).

The Steps to Freedom in Christ do not set you free. *Who* sets you free is Christ, and *what* sets you free is your response to Him in repentance and faith. These steps are just a tool to help you submit to God and resist the devil (James 4:7). Then you can start living a fruitful life by recognizing who you are in Christ, spending time with Him, and becoming the person He created you to be. Many Christians will be able to work through these steps on their own and discover the wonderful freedom that Christ purchased for them on the cross. Then they will experience the peace of God that surpasses all understanding, and it will guard their hearts and their minds (see Philippians 4:7).

The chances of that happening and the possibility of maintaining that freedom will be greatly increased if you first read *Stomping Out the Darkness* and *The Bondage Breaker Youth Edition*. Many Christians in our western world need to understand the reality of the spiritual world and our relationship to it. Some can't read these books or even the Bible with understanding because of the battle that is going on for their minds. They may need the help of someone who has been trained to take them through the Steps to Freedom in Christ.*

It would be best if everyone had a pastor, youth pastor, or counselor who would help them go through this process because it is just applying the wisdom of James 5:16: "Confess your sins to one another, and pray for one another so that you may be healed. The effective prayer of a righteous man can accomplish much." Another person can prayerfully support you.

Gaining Freedom

Spiritual freedom is meant for every Christian, young or old. Being "free in Christ" is to have the desire and power to worship God and do His will. It is to know God's truth, believe God's truth, and live according to God's truth. It is to walk with God in the power of the Holy Spirit and to experience a life of love, joy, and peace. It is not a life of perfection, but of progress! All these qualities may not be yours now, but they are meant for everyone who is in Christ.

If you have received Christ as your Savior, He has already set you free through His victory over sin and death on the cross. However, experiencing our freedom in Christ through repentance and faith and maintaining our life of freedom in Christ are two

---

* The theological and practical process of taking others through the Steps to Freedom is explained in the book *Leading Teens to Freedom in Christ*.

different issues. Establishing people as free in Christ makes it possible for them to walk by faith according to what God says is true and live by the power of the Holy Spirit and not carry out the desires of the flesh (Galatians 5:16).

However, if freedom is not a constant reality for you, it may be because you do not understand how Christ can help you deal with the pain of your past or the problems of your present life. It is your responsibility as one who knows Christ to do whatever is needed to maintain a right relationship with God and others. Your eternal life is not at stake—you are safe and secure in Christ. But your daily victory *is* at stake if you fail to understand who you are in Christ and live according to that truth.

We've got great news for you! You are not a helpless victim caught between two nearly equal but opposite heavenly superpowers, God and Satan. Only God is all-powerful, always present, and all-knowing. Sometimes, however, the presence and power of sin and evil in our lives can seem more real to us than the presence and power of God. But that is part of Satan's tricky lie. Satan is a deceiver, and he wants you to think he is stronger than he really is. But he is also a defeated enemy, and you are in Christ, the Victor.

Understanding who God is and who you are in Christ are the two most important factors in determining your daily victory over sin and Satan. The greatest causes of spiritual defeat are false beliefs about God, not understanding who you are as a child of God, and making Satan out to be as powerful and present as God is.

A Battle for Your Mind

This battle is for your mind. You may experience nagging thoughts like "this isn't going to work" or "God doesn't love me." These thoughts are lies, planted in your mind by deceiving spirits. If you believe them, you will really struggle as you work through these steps. These opposing thoughts can control you only if you believe them.

If you are working through these steps by yourself, don't pay attention to any lying or threatening thoughts in your mind. If you're working through the steps with a youth pastor, pastor, or counselor (which we strongly recommend), then share any opposing thought with that person. Whenever you uncover a lie and choose to believe the truth, the power of Satan is broken.

You must cooperate with the person who is trying to help you. Do this by sharing what is going on inside your mind. Also, if you experience any physical discomfort (for example, headache, nausea, tightness in the throat, and so on), don't be alarmed. Just tell the person you are with so he or she can pray for you.

As believers in Christ, we can pray with authority to stop any interference by Satan. Here is a prayer and declaration to get you started. All prayers and declarations throughout the steps should be read out loud.

Prayer

Dear heavenly Father, we know that You are always here and present in our lives. You are the only all-knowing, all-powerful, ever-present God. We desperately need You because without Jesus we can do nothing. We believe the Bible because it tells us what is really true. We refuse to believe the lies of Satan. We stand in the truth that all authority in heaven and on earth has been given to the resurrected Christ. Because we are in Christ, we share His authority in order to make followers of Jesus and set captives free.

We ask You to protect our thoughts and minds and lead us into all truth. We choose to submit to the Holy Spirit. Please reveal to our minds everything You want to deal with today. We ask for and trust in Your wisdom. We pray for Your complete protection over us. In Jesus' name, amen.

Declaration

> *In the name and the authority of the Lord Jesus Christ, we command Satan and all evil spirits to let go of (<u>name</u>) in order that (<u>name</u>) can be free to know and choose to do the will of God. As children of God, seated with Christ in the heavenlies, we agree that every enemy of the Lord Jesus Christ be bound to silence. We say to Satan and all of his evil workers that you cannot inflict any pain or in any way stop or hinder God's will from being done today in (<u>name</u>)'s life.*

The Seven Steps

Following are seven steps to help you be free from your past. You will cover the areas where Satan most often takes advantage of us and where strongholds have been built. Christ purchased your victory when He shed His blood for you on the cross. You will experience your freedom when you make the choice to believe, confess, forgive, renounce, and forsake. No one can do that for you. The battle for your mind can only be won as you *personally* choose truth.

As you go through these Steps to Freedom in Christ, remember that Satan cannot read your mind, thus he won't obey your thoughts. Only God knows what you are thinking. As you go through each Step, it is important that you submit to God inwardly and resist the devil by reading each prayer *out loud*—verbally renouncing, forgiving, confessing, and so on.

You are going to be taking a thorough look at your life in order to get radically right with God. If it turns out that you have another kind of problem—not covered in these steps—that is negatively affecting your life, you will have lost nothing. If you are open and honest during this time, you will greatly benefit anyway by becoming right with God and close to Him again.

May the Lord greatly touch your life during this time. He will give you the strength to make it through. It is essential that you work through *all* seven steps, so don't allow yourself to become discouraged and give up. Remember, the freedom that Christ purchased for all believers on the cross is meant for *you!* *

Step 1: Counterfeit vs. Real

The first step toward experiencing your freedom in Christ is to renounce (to reject and turn your back on) all past, present, and future participation in satanic-inspired occult practices, things done in secret, and non-Christian religions. You must renounce any activity and group which denies Jesus Christ, offers direction through any source other than the absolute authority of the written Word of God, or requires secret initiations, ceremonies, promises, or pacts (covenants). Begin with the following prayer:

> *Dear heavenly Father, I ask You to guard my heart and my mind and to reveal to me anything that I have done or that anyone has done to me which is spiritually wrong. Reveal to my mind any and all involvement I have knowingly or unknowingly had with cult or occult practices, or false teachers, or both. I ask this in Jesus' name, amen.*

Even if you took part in something as a game or as a joke, you need to renounce it. Satan will try to take advantage of anything he can in our lives. Even if you just stood by and watched others do it, you need to renounce it. Even if you did it just once and had no idea it was evil, still you need to renounce it. You want to remove any and every possible foothold of Satan in your life.

---

* If you are taking someone through the Steps to Freedom, you may want to turn to appendix A to go over the events of their life so that you understand the areas that might need to be dealt with. If a Confidential Personal Inventory has been filled out, you may want to review it at this time.

Non-Christian Spiritual Experiences Checklist

(Please check all those that apply to you.)

- ❐ Out-of-body experience (astral projection)
- ❐ Bloody Mary and other occult games
- ❐ Table-lifting or body-lifting (Light as a Feather)
- ❐ Magic Eight Ball
- ❐ Ouija board
- ❐ Using spells or curses
- ❐ Chants or mantras
- ❐ Mental control of others
- ❐ Automatic writing
- ❐ Spirit guides
- ❐ Fortune telling or tarot cards
- ❐ Palm-reading or tea-leaf–reading
- ❐ Astrology or horoscopes
- ❐ Hypnosis
- ❐ Seances
- ❐ Black or white magic
- ❐ Dungeons and Dragons (or other fantasy role-playing games like Magic, and so on)
- ❐ Video or computer games involving occult powers or cruel violence
- ❐ Blood pacts or cutting yourself on purpose
- ❐ Objects of worship or good-luck charms
- ❐ Superstitions
- ❐ Sexual spirits
- ❐ New Age medicine (use of crystals)

- ❏ Idols of rock stars, actors or actresses, sports heroes, and others
- ❏ Masons
- ❏ Christian Science
- ❏ Science of Mind
- ❏ Science of Creative Intelligence
- ❏ The Way International
- ❏ Unification Church (Moonies)
- ❏ The Forum (est)
- ❏ Church of the Living Word
- ❏ Children of God (Children of Love)
- ❏ Mormonism
- ❏ Jehovah's Witnesses (Watchtower)
- ❏ Scientology
- ❏ Unitarianism
- ❏ Roy Masters
- ❏ Silva Mind Control
- ❏ Transcendental Meditation (TM)
- ❏ Yoga
- ❏ Hare Krishna
- ❏ Baha'ism
- ❏ New Age
- ❏ Islam
- ❏ Black Muslim beliefs
- ❏ Martial arts (involving Eastern mysticism, meditation, or devotion to *sensei*)
- ❏ Buddhism (including Zen)

❒ Rosicrucianism
❒ Native American spirit worship
❒ Hinduism
❒ Other:

Note: This is not a complete list. If you have any doubts about an activity not included here, renounce your involvement in it. If it has come to mind here, trust that the Lord wants you to renounce it.

List below those things that especially glorified Satan, caused fear or nightmares, or were gruesomely violent.

❒ Anti-Christian movies:

❒ Anti-Christian music:

❒ Anti-Christian TV shows or video games:

❒ Anti-Christian books, magazines, and comics:

Here are some additional questions to help you become aware of other things you may need to renounce.

    1. Have you ever heard or seen or felt an evil spiritual presence in your room or somewhere else?

    2. Do you have, or have you had, an imaginary friend, spirit guide, or angel offering you guidance and companionship?

    3. Have you ever heard voices in your head or had repetitious negative, nagging thoughts such as "I'm dumb," "I'm ugly," "Nobody loves me," "I can't do anything right," and so on—as if a conversation were going on in your head? Explain.

    4. Have you ever consulted a medium, spiritist, or channeler?

5. What other spiritual experiences have you had that would be considered out of the ordinary (supernatural knowledge of something, special spiritual gifts, contact with aliens, and so on)?

6. Have you ever been involved in satanic worship of any kind or attended a concert at which Satan was the focus?

7. Have you ever made a vow or pact?

Once you have completed the above checklist, confess and renounce each item you were involved in by praying aloud the following prayer (repeat the prayer separately for each item on your list):

*Lord, I confess that I have participated in _____.
I renounce any and all influence and involvement with _____, and thank You that in Christ I am forgiven.*

If you (or the individual going through the Steps to Freedom) have been involved in any Satanic ritual or heavy occult activity (or you suspect it because of blocked memories, severe and recurring nightmares, or severe sexual bondage), you need to say out loud the special renunciations and affirmations in appendix B at the end of the Steps.

Step 2: Deception vs. Truth

God's Word is true, and we need to accept the truth deep in our hearts (Psalm 51:6). What God says is true whether we feel it is true or not!

Jesus is the truth (John 14:6), the Holy Spirit is the Spirit of truth (John 16:13), and the Word of God is truth (John 17:17). We ought to speak the truth in love (Ephesians 4:15). The believer in Christ has no business deceiving others either by lying, exaggerating, telling little lies, or stretching the truth. Satan is the father of lies (John 8:44), and he seeks to keep people in bondage through deception (Revelation 12:9; 2 Timothy 2:26). But it is the truth in Jesus that sets us free (John 8:32-34).

We will find real joy and freedom when we stop living a lie and walk openly in the truth. After confessing his sin, King David wrote, "How blessed is the man…in whose spirit there is no deceit!" (Psalm 32:2).

How can we find the strength to walk in the light (I John 1:7)? When we are sure that God loves and accepts us, we can be free to own up to our sin, face reality, and not run or hide from painful circumstances.

Start this step by praying the following prayer out loud. Don't let any opposing thoughts such as "This is a waste of time" or "I wish I could believe this stuff but I just can't" keep you from praying and choosing the truth. Belief is a choice. If you choose to believe what you feel, then Satan, the father of lies, will keep you in bondage. You must choose to believe what God says, regardless of what your feelings might say. Even if you have a hard time doing so, pray the following prayer:

> *Dear heavenly Father, I know You want me to face the truth. I know that I must be honest with You. I know that choosing to believe the truth will set me free. I have been deceived by*

Satan, and I have deceived myself. I thought I could hide from You, but You see everything and still love me.

I pray in the name of the Lord Jesus Christ, asking You to rebuke all of Satan's demons that are deceiving me. By faith I have received You into my life and am now seated with Christ in the heavenlies. I acknowledge that I have the responsibility to submit to You, and the authority to resist the devil—and when I do, he will flee from me.

Since You accept me just as I am in Christ, I can be free to face my sin. I ask for the Holy Spirit to guide me into all truth. I ask You to "search me, O God, and know my heart; try me and know my anxious thoughts; and see if there be any hurtful way in me, and lead me in the everlasting way." In the name of Jesus I pray, amen.

(See Ephesians 2:6; James 4:7; Psalm 139:23-24.)

There are many ways in which Satan, "the god of this world" (2 Corinthians 4:4), seeks to deceive us. Just as he did with Eve, the devil tries to convince us to rely on ourselves and to try to get our needs met through the world around us, rather than trusting in our Father in heaven.

Ways You Can Be Deceived by the World

- ❐ Believing that accumulating money and possessions will bring happiness (Matthew 13:22; 1 Timothy 6:10)

- ❐ Believing that eating food and drinking alcohol without restraint will make me happy (Proverbs 20:1; 23:19-21)

- ❐ Believing that a sexy, attractive body and personality will get me what I want or need (Proverbs 31:10; 1 Peter 3:3-4)

❏ Believing that gratifying sexual lust will bring true fulfillment (Ephesians 4:22; 1 Peter 2:11)

❏ Believing that I can sin and get away with it—and not have it affect my heart and character (Hebrews 3:12-13)

❏ Believing that my needs cannot be totally taken care of by God (2 Corinthians 11:2-4,13-15)

❏ Believing that I am important and strong—and I can do whatever I want and no one can touch me! (Obadiah 3; 1 Peter 5:5; Proverbs 16:18)

Use the following prayer of confession for each item above that you have believed. Pray through each item separately.

Lord, I confess that I have been deceived by _____. I thank You for Your forgiveness, and I commit myself to believing only Your truth. Amen.

It is important to know that in addition to being deceived by the world, false teachers, and deceiving spirits, you can also fool yourself. Now that you are alive in Christ, forgiven, and totally accepted, you don't need to live a lie or defend yourself like you used to. Christ is now your truth and defense.

Ways You Can Deceive Yourself

❏ Hearing God's Word but not always doing it (James 1:22)

❏ Saying I have no sin (1 John 1:8)

❏ Thinking I am something I'm not (Galatians 6:3)

❏ Thinking I am wise in the things of the world (1 Corinthians 3:18-19)

❒ Thinking I can be a good Christian but still hurt others by what I say (James 1:26)

❒ Thinking my secret sin will hurt only me but will not hurt others (for example, pornography, voyeurism, hatred) (Exodus 20:4-5)

Use the following prayer of confession for each item above that you have believed. Pray through each item separately.

> *Lord, I confess that I have deceived myself by* _____.
> *I thank You for Your forgiveness and commit myself to believing Your truth.*

Wrong Ways of Defending Yourself

❒ Refusing to face the bad things that have happened to me (denial of reality)

❒ Escaping from the real world through daydreaming, TV, movies, computer or video games, music, and so on (fantasy)

❒ Withdrawing from people to avoid rejection (emotional insulation)

❒ Reverting (going back) to a less threatening time of life (regression)

❒ Taking out frustrations on others (displaced anger)

❒ Blaming others for my problems (projection)

❒ Making excuses for poor behavior (rationalization)

Use the following prayer of confession for each item above that you have participated in. Pray through each item separately.

> *Lord, I confess that I have defended myself wrongly by*
> *_____. I thank You for Your forgiveness and*
> *commit myself to trusting in You to defend and protect me.*

Choosing the truth may be difficult if you have been living a lie and have been deceived for some time. The Christian needs only one defense—Jesus. Knowing that you are completely forgiven and accepted as God's child sets you free to face reality and declare your total dependence upon Him.

If you are not experiencing a close relationship with your heavenly Father, it may be because of lies that you have believed about Him. Turn to appendix C and say out loud the renunciations and affirmations listed there.

If you are struggling to walk by faith, it may be because of the fears that plague your life. In order to begin to experience freedom from the bondage of fear turn to appendix D and pray the prayers there.

Faith Must Be Based on the Truth of God's Word

Faith is the biblical response to the truth, and believing the truth is a choice we can all make. If you say, "I want to believe God, but I just can't," you are being deceived. Of course you can believe God, because what God says is always true.

Faith is something you decide to do, whether or not you feel like doing it. Believing the truth doesn't make it true, however. *It's true—therefore, we believe it.*

The New Age movement twists the truth by saying we create reality through what we believe. We can't create reality with our minds. We can only *face* reality with our minds. Simply "having faith" is not the key issue here. It's what or who you believe in that makes the difference. You see, everybody believes in something, and everybody lives according to what he or she believes. The question is, is the object of your faith trustworthy? If what you believe is not true, then how you live will not be right.

For centuries, Christians have known that it is important to declare to others what they believe. Read aloud the following "Statement of Truth," thinking about the words as you read them. Read it every day for several weeks. This will help you renew your mind and replace any lies you have believed with the truth.

Statement of Truth

1. *I believe there is only one true and living God (Exodus 20:2-3), who is the Father, Son, and Holy Spirit. He is worthy of all honor, praise, and glory. I believe that He made all things and holds all things together (Colossians 1:16-17).*

2. *I recognize Jesus Christ as the Messiah, the Word who became flesh and lived with us (John 1:1,14). I believe He came to destroy the works of Satan (1 John 3:8) and that He disarmed the rulers and authorities and made a public display of them, having triumphed over them (Colossians 2:15).*

3. *I believe that God showed His love for me by having Jesus die for me, even though I was sinful (Romans 5:8). I believe that God rescued me from the dark power of Satan and brought me into the kingdom of His Son, who forgives my sins and sets me free (Colossians 1:13-14).*

4. *I believe I am spiritually strong because Jesus is my strength. I have authority to stand against Satan because I am God's child (1 John 3:1-3). I believe that I was saved by the grace of God through faith, that it was a gift and not the result of any works of mine (Ephesians 2:8-9).*

5. I choose to be strong in the Lord and in the strength of His might (Ephesians 6:10). I put no confidence in the flesh (Philippians 3:3) because my weapons of spiritual battle are not of the flesh but are powerful through God for the tearing down of Satan's strongholds (2 Corinthians 10:4). I put on the whole armor of God (Ephesians 6:10-20), and I resolve to stand firm in my faith and resist the evil one (1 Peter 5:8-9).

6. I believe that apart from Christ I can do nothing (John 15:5), yet I can do all things through Him who strengthens me (Philippians 4:13). Therefore, I choose to rely totally on Christ. I choose to abide in Christ in order to bear much fruit and glorify the Lord (John 15:8). I announce to Satan that Jesus is my Lord (1 Corinthians 12:3), and I reject any counterfeit gifts or works of Satan in my life.

7. I believe that the truth will set me free (John 8:32). I stand against Satan's lies by taking every thought captive in obedience to Christ (2 Corinthians 10:5). I believe that the Bible is the only reliable guide for my life (2 Timothy 3:15-16). I choose to speak the truth in love (Ephesians 4:15).

8. I choose to present my body as an instrument of righteousness, a living and holy sacrifice, and to renew my mind with God's Word (Romans 6:13; 12:1-2). I have put off the old self with its evil practices and have put on the new self (Colossians 3:9-10). I am a new creation in Christ (2 Corinthians 5:17).

9. I trust my heavenly Father to direct my life and give me power to live by the Holy Spirit (Ephesians 5:18), so that He can guide me into all truth (John 16:13). I believe He will give me strength to live above sin and not carry out

the desires of my flesh. I crucify the flesh, and choose to be led by the Holy Spirit and obey Him (Galatians 5:16,24).

10. *I renounce all selfish goals and choose the greatest goal of love (I Timothy 1:5). I choose to obey the two greatest commandments: to love the Lord my God with all my heart, soul, and mind, and to love my neighbor as myself (Matthew 22:37-39).*

11. *I believe that Jesus has all authority in heaven and on earth (Matthew 28:18) and that He rules over everything (Colossians 2:10). I believe that Satan and his demons have been defeated by Christ and are subject to me since I am a member of Christ's body (Ephesians 1:19-23). So, I obey the command to submit to God and to resist the devil (James 4:7), and I command Satan, by the authority of the Lord Jesus Christ, to leave my presence.*

Step 3: Bitterness vs. Forgiveness

When you fail to forgive those who hurt you, you become a wide-open target for Satan. God commands us to forgive others as we have been forgiven (Ephesians 4:32). You need to obey this command so that Satan can't take advantage of you (2 Corinthians 2:10-11). Christians are to forgive others and show them mercy because our heavenly Father has shown mercy to us (Luke 6:36). Ask God to bring to your mind the name of those people you need to forgive by praying the following prayer out loud. (Remember to let this prayer come from your heart as well as your mouth!)

Dear heavenly Father, I thank You for Your great kindness and patience, which have led me to turn from my sins. I know I have not always been completely kind, patient, and loving toward those who have hurt me. I have had bad thoughts and feelings toward them.

I ask You to bring to my mind all the people I need to forgive. I ask You to bring to the surface all my painful memories so I can choose to forgive these people from my heart. I pray this in the precious name of Jesus, who has forgiven me and who will heal me from my hurts. Amen.

(See Romans 2:4; Matthew 18:35.)

On a sheet of paper, make a list of the people who come to your mind. At this point, don't question whether you need to forgive a certain person or not. If a name comes to your mind, write it down. Finally, write "myself" at the bottom of the list. Forgiving yourself means accepting God's cleansing and forgiveness.

Also write "thoughts against God." We sometimes harbor angry thoughts toward God. We can expect or even demand that He act in a certain way in our lives, and when He doesn't do what we want in the way we want, we can get angry. Those feelings can become a wall between us and God, and even though we don't actually need to forgive Him (because He is perfect), we do need to let those feelings go.

- *Forgiveness is not forgetting.* People who want to be able to forget all their pain before they get around to forgiving someone usually find they cannot. God commands us to forgive now. Confusion sometimes arises because Scripture says that God "will remember no more our sins" (Hebrews 10:17). But God knows everything and can't "forget"—as if He had no memory of our sin. His promise is that He will never use our past against us (Psalm 103:10-12).

  The key issue is this: We may not be able to forget our past, but we can be free from it by forgiving others. When we bring up the past and use it against others, we are showing that we have not yet forgiven them (Mark 11:25).

- *Forgiveness is a choice, a decision of the will.* Since God requires us to forgive, it is something we can do. Forgiveness seems hard because it goes against our sense of what is right and fair. We naturally want revenge for the things we have suffered. But we are told by God never to take our own revenge (Romans 12:19).

  You might be thinking, *Why should I let them off the hook?* And that is exactly the problem! As long as you do not forgive, you are still hooked to those who hurt you! You are still chained to your past. *By forgiving, you let them off your hook, but they are not off God's hook.* We must trust Him to deal with the other person justly, fairly, and mercifully, something we cannot do.

  You say, "But you don't know how much this person hurt me." But until you let go of your hate and anger, they will continue to be able to hurt you. You finally stop the pain by forgiving them. *You forgive for your sake, so that you can be free.* Forgiveness is mainly an issue of obedience between you and God. God wants you to be free; this is the only way.

- *Forgiveness is agreeing to live with the consequences of another person's sin.* Forgiveness costs you something. You choose to pay the price for the evil you forgive. *But you will live with the consequences whether you want to or not.* Your only choice is whether you will do so in the bondage of bitterness or in the freedom of forgiveness.

  Of course, Jesus took the eternal consequences of *all* sin upon Himself. God "made Him who knew no sin to be sin on our behalf so that we might become the righteousness of God in Him" (2 Corinthians 5:21). We need, however, to accept the temporary consequences of what was done to us. But no one truly forgives without suffering the pain of another's sin. That can seem unfair, and we may wonder, Where's the justice? It is found at the cross, which makes forgiveness legally and morally right. As those who crucified Him mocked Him and jeered at Him, Jesus prayed, "Father, forgive them; for they do not know what they are doing" (Luke 23:34).

- *Forgive from your heart.* Allow God to bring to the surface the mental agony, emotional pain, and feelings of hurt toward those who hurt you. If your forgiveness does not reach down to the emotional core of your life, it will be incomplete. Too often we try to bury the pain inside us, making it hard to get in touch with how we really feel. Though we may not know how, or even want, to bring our feelings to the surface, God does. Let God bring the pain to the surface so that He can deal with it. This is where God's gentle healing process begins.

- *Forgiveness is the decision not to use someone's offense against them.* It is not unusual for us to remember a past, hurtful event and find the anger and hate we felt returning. It is tempting to bring up the issue with the one who hurt us in order to make them feel bad. But we must choose to take that thought of revenge captive to the obedience of Christ, and choose to maintain forgiveness.

This doesn't mean that you must continue to put up with the future sins of others. God does not tolerate sin and neither should you. Nor should you put yourself in the position of being continually abused and hurt by the sins of others. You need to take a stand against sin while continuing to forgive those who hurt you.

- *Don't wait to forgive until you feel like forgiving.* You will never get there. Your emotions will begin to heal once you have obeyed God's command to forgive. Satan will have lost his power over you in that area, and God's healing touch will take over. For now, it is *freedom* that will be gained, not necessarily a feeling.

As you pray, God may bring to mind painful memories that you had totally forgotten. Let Him do this, even if it hurts. God wants you to be free—forgiving these people is the only way. Don't try to excuse the offender's behavior, even if it is someone close to you.

Remember, forgiveness is dealing with your own pain and leaving the other person to deal with God. Good feelings will follow in time. Freeing yourself from the past is the critical issue right now.

Don't say, "Lord, please help me to forgive." He is already helping you and will be with you all the way through the process. Don't say, "Lord, I want to forgive," because that bypasses the hard choice we have to make. Say, "Lord, I forgive."

As you move down your list, stay with each individual until you are sure you have dealt with all the remembered pain, everything the person did that hurt you, and how it made you feel (rejected, unloved, unworthy, dirty, and so on).

It's time to begin. For each person on your list, pray aloud,

> *Lord, I forgive (<u>name the person</u>) for (<u>say what they did to hurt you</u>—be specific) even though it made me feel (<u>share the painful memories or feelings</u>).*

Once you have dealt with every offense that has come to your mind and you have honestly expressed how that person hurt you, then conclude by praying,

> *Lord, I choose not to hold any of these things against (__name__) any longer. I thank You for setting me free from the bondage of my bitterness toward him or her. I choose now to ask You to bless (__name__). In Jesus' name, amen.*

Step 4: Rebellion vs. Submission

We live in rebellious times. Often young people today don't respect people that God has placed in authority over them. You may have a problem living in submission to authority. You can easily be deceived into thinking that those in authority over you are robbing you of your freedom. In reality, however, God has placed them there for your protection.

Rebelling against God and His authorities is serious business. It gives Satan an opportunity to attack you. Submission is the only solution. God requires more of you, however, than just the outward appearance of submission. He wants you to sincerely submit to your authorities (especially parents) from the heart. Your commanding general, the Lord Jesus Christ, is telling you to "get into ranks and follow Me!" He promises that He will not lead you into temptation, but will deliver you from evil (Matthew 6:13).

The Bible makes it clear that we have two main responsibilities toward those in authority over us: to pray for them and to submit to them. Pray the following prayer out loud from your heart.

> *Dear heavenly Father, You have said in the Bible that rebellion is the same thing as witchcraft, and being self-willed is like serving false gods. I know that I have disobeyed and*

rebelled in my heart against You and those You have placed in authority over me.

I thank You for Your forgiveness for my rebellion. By the shed blood of the Lord Jesus Christ, I pray that all doors that I have opened to evil spirits through my rebellion would now be closed. I pray that You will show me all the ways I have been rebellious. I now choose to adopt a submissive spirit and servant's heart. In Jesus' precious name, I pray. Amen.

(See 1 Samuel 15:23.)

Rebellion will often be expressed through an uncooperative attitude and a critical spirit. The following actions are some possible results of rebellion. Check those that apply to the different authorities in your life.

- ❐ Refusing to obey or follow legitimate instructions
- ❐ Ignoring instructions or requirements, or adjusting them to suit myself
- ❐ Believing it is my right to criticize those in authority over me
- ❐ Making critical statements about authority figures
- ❐ Rejecting the advice of others who have experience and wisdom
- ❐ Finding fault easily with a person, group, or organization, particularly those in authority
- ❐ Reading a negative bias into things that others say or do
- ❐ Passing along negative information to others who are not part of the problem or solution
- ❐ Withdrawing from communications with others (often shown by short, clipped responses or silence)

❑ Speaking disrespectfully to another person or about another person

❑ Having to have the last words in a conversation

Lord, I now agree with You that I have been rebellious by _____. Thank you for forgiving me for my rebellion.

We are all told to submit to one another as equals in Christ (Ephesians 5:21). In addition, however, God uses specific lines of authority to protect us and give order to our daily lives. Being under authority is an act of faith! By submitting, we are trusting God to work through His lines of authority. Check those authorities you have been rebellious to.

❑ Civil government (including traffic laws, drinking laws, and so on) (Romans 13:1-7; 1 Peter 2:13-17)

❑ Parents, stepparents, or legal guardians (Ephesians 6:1-3)

❑ Teachers, coaches, or school officials (Romans 13:1-4)

❑ Your boss (1 Peter 2:18-23)

❑ Husband (1 Peter 3:1-4) or wife (Ephesians 5:21; 1 Peter 3:7). [Note to husbands: Take a moment and ask the Lord if your lack of love for your wife could be fostering a rebellious spirit within her. If so, confess it now as a violation of Ephesians 5:22-23.]

❑ Church leaders (pastor, youth pastor, Sunday school teacher) (Hebrews 13:17)

❑ God Himself (Daniel 9:5,9)

Use the following prayer to ask the Lord to forgive you for those times you have been rebellious in attitude or actions.

> *Lord, I agree with You that I have been rebellious toward (name), by (say what you did specifically). Thank You for forgiving my rebellion. I choose to be submissive and to treat others with kindness and respect. In Jesus' name, amen.*

At times, parents, teachers, employers, and other authority figures may abuse their authority and break the laws that are ordained by God for the protection of innocent people. In those cases, you need to seek help from a *higher* authority for your protection. The laws in your state may require you to report such abuse to the police or other protective agencies. If there is continuing abuse (physical, mental, emotional, or sexual) at home or anywhere else, counseling may be needed to change the situation. If someone abuses their authority by asking you to break God's law or compromise yourself, you need to obey God rather than man (Acts 4:19-20).

Step 5: Pride vs. Humility

Pride is a killer. Pride says, "I can do it! I can get myself out of this mess without God or anyone else's help." Oh no, you can't! We absolutely need God, and we desperately need each other. Paul wrote that we "worship in the Spirit of God and glory in Christ Jesus and put no confidence in the flesh" (Philippians 3:3).

Humility is confidence properly placed in God. We are to be "strong in the Lord and in the strength of His might" (Ephesians 6:10). James 4:6-10 and 1 Peter 5:1-10 tell us that spiritual problems will follow when we are proud. Use the following prayer to express your commitment to live humbly before God.

> *Dear heavenly Father, You have said that pride goes before destruction and an arrogant spirit before stumbling. I confess that I have been thinking mainly of myself and not of others. I have not denied myself, picked up my cross daily, and*

followed You. As a result, I have given ground to the enemy in my life. I have believed that I could be successful by living according to my own power and resources.

I now confess that I have sinned against You by placing my will before Yours and by centering my life around myself instead of You. I renounce my pride and my selfishness, and I close any doors I've opened in my life or physical body to the enemies of the Lord Jesus Christ. I choose to rely on the Holy Spirit's power and guidance so that I can do Your will.

I give my heart to You and stand against all of Satan's attacks. I ask You to show me how to live for others. I now choose to make others more important than myself and to make You the most important Person of all in my life. Please show me specifically now the ways in which I have lived pridefully. I ask this in the name of my Lord, Jesus Christ, amen.

(See Proverbs 16:18; Matthew 16:24;
Romans 12:10; Matthew 6:33.)

Having made that commitment in prayer, now allow God to show you any specific areas of your life where you have been prideful.

❐ Having a stronger desire to do my will than God's

❐ Relying on my own strengths and abilities rather than on God's

❐ Thinking my ideas are better than other people's

❐ Wanting to control how others act, rather than develop self-control

❐ Considering myself more important than others

❐ Having a tendency to think I don't need people

❐ Finding it difficult to admit when I am wrong

❒ Being a people-pleaser rather than a God-pleaser

❒ Being overconcerned about getting credit for doing good things

❒ Thinking I am more humble than others

❒ Thinking I am smarter than my parents

❒ Feeling that my needs are more important than other people's needs

❒ Considering myself better than others because of my academic, artistic, or athletic abilities and accomplishments

❒ Other:

For each of the above areas that has been true in your life, pray out loud,

> *Lord, I agree that I have been prideful in the area of*
> *_____ . Thank You for forgiving me for this pridefulness. I choose to humble myself and place all my confidence in You. Amen.*

Prejudice and Bigotry

Two other forms of pride are prejudice and bigotry, which are all too common today. At first, you might think that these attitudes couldn't be true of you. But if you have any awareness of prideful attitudes toward others, this is a good reason to prayerfully allow God to search your heart and bring to the surface anything that needs to be taken care of. You can find a prayer and renunciation dealing with these issues in appendix E at the end of the Steps.

Step 6: Bondage vs. Freedom

The next step to freedom deals with the sins that have become habits in your life. If you have been caught in the vicious cycle of "sin-confess-sin-confess," realize that the road to victory is "sin-confess-*resist*" (James 4:7).

Habitual sin often requires help from a trusted brother or sister in Christ. James 5:16 says, "Confess your sins to one another, and pray for one another so that you may be healed. The effective prayer of a righteous man can accomplish much." Seek out a stronger Christian who will lift you up in prayer and hold you accountable in your areas of weakness.

Sometimes the assurance of 1 John 1:9 is sufficient: "If we confess our sins, He is faithful and righteous to forgive us our sins and to cleanse us from all unrighteousness." Remember, confession is not saying "I'm sorry"—it's openly admitting, "I did it." Whether you need the help of others or just the accountability of God, pray the following prayer out loud:

> *Dear heavenly Father, You have told us to put on the Lord Jesus Christ and make no provision for the flesh in regard to its lusts. I agree that I have given in to sinful desires which wage war against my soul.*
>
> *I thank You that in Christ my sins are forgiven. But I have broken Your holy law and given the devil an opportunity to wage war in my body. I come before Your presence now to admit these sins and to seek Your cleansing so that I may be freed from the bondage of sin. I now ask You to reveal to my mind the ways that I have broken Your moral law and grieved the Holy Spirit. In Jesus' precious name I pray, amen.*
>
> (See Romans 13:14; 1 Peter 2:11; Romans 6:12-13; James 4:1; 1 Peter 5:8; 1 John 1:9.)

There are many habitual sins that can control us. The following list contains some of the more common sins of the flesh. Look through the following list and ask the Holy Spirit to reveal to your mind which ones from the past or the present you need to confess. He may bring to mind others that are not here.

For each one God reveals, pray the following prayer of confession from the heart. (Note: Sexual sins, eating disorders, substance abuse, abortion, suicidal tendencies, and perfectionism will be dealt with later.)

- ❐ Stealing (shoplifting)
- ❐ Lying
- ❐ Fighting
- ❐ Quarreling or arguing
- ❐ Hatred
- ❐ Jealousy, envy
- ❐ Anger
- ❐ Complaining and criticism
- ❐ Depression or hopelessness
- ❐ Impure thoughts
- ❐ Eagerness for lustful pleasure
- ❐ Cheating
- ❐ Gossip or slander
- ❐ Procrastination (putting things off)
- ❐ Swearing
- ❐ Greed or materialism
- ❐ Apathy or laziness
- ❐ Other:

Lord, I now admit that I have committed the sin of _____. I thank You for Your forgiveness and cleansing. I turn away from this sin and turn to You, Lord. Strengthen me by Your Holy Spirit to obey You. In Jesus' name, amen.

Wrong Sexual Use of Our Body

It is our responsibility to take control over sin in our bodies. We must not use our bodies or someone else's as an instrument of unrighteousness (Romans 6:12-13). If you are or have been struggling with sexual sins (such as pornography, masturbation, heavy petting, heavy kissing, oral sex, same-sex relationships, voyeurism, phone sex, computer or Internet sex, or sexual intercourse), pray as follows:

Lord, I ask You to reveal to my mind every sexual use of my body as an instrument of unrighteousness. In Jesus' precious name I pray, amen.

As the Lord brings to your mind every wrong sexual use of your body, whether it was done to you (rape, incest, any sexual abuse) or willingly by you, renounce *every* occasion:

Lord, I renounce (<u>name the specific use of your body</u>) with (<u>name the person involved</u>), and I ask You to break that sinful bond with (<u>name</u>).

After you have completed this exercise, commit your body to the Lord by praying out loud from your heart,

Lord, I renounce all these uses of my body as an instrument of unrighteousness, and I ask you to break all bondages that

Satan has brought into my life through my involvement. I admit my participation.

Lord, I choose to present my eyes, my mouth, my mind, my hands and feet—my whole body—to You as instruments of righteousness. I now present my body to You as a living sacrifice, holy and acceptable to You, and I choose to reserve the sexual use of my body for marriage only.

I reject the lie of Satan that my body is not clean, or that it is dirty or in any way unacceptable to You as a result of my past sexual experiences. Lord, I thank You that You have totally cleansed and forgiven me, and that You love me just as I am. Therefore, I can accept myself and my body as cleansed in Your eyes. In Jesus' name, amen.

(See Hebrews 13:4.)

If you have struggled with, or are currently struggling with, homosexuality, suicidal tendencies, eating disorders, cutting yourself, substance abuse, or drivenness and perfectionism, or if you have had an abortion or have not assumed your responsibilities for an unborn child, turn to appendix F and pray the special prayers there.

Step 7: Curses vs. Blessings

The last step to freedom is to renounce the sins of your ancestors and any curses that may have been placed on you. In giving the Ten Commandments, God said,

> You shall not make for yourself an idol, or any likeness of what is in heaven above or on the earth beneath or in the water under the earth. You shall not worship them or serve them; for I, the LORD your God, am a jealous God, visiting the iniquity of the fathers on the children, on the third and fourth generations of those who hate Me (Exodus 20:4-5).

Iniquities can be passed on from one generation to the next if you don't renounce the sins of your ancestors and claim your new spiritual heritage in Christ. You are not guilty for the sin of any ancestor, but because of his or her sin, you may be vulnerable to Satan's attack.

Because of the fall, certain strengths or weaknesses are born into you, and you are influenced by the physical and spiritual atmosphere in which you have been raised. These things can work together to cause you to struggle with a particular sin.

Ask the Lord to show you specifically what sins are characteristic of your family by praying the following prayer:

> *Dear heavenly Father, I ask You to reveal to my mind all the sins of my ancestors that are being passed down through family lines. I want to be free from those influences and walk in my new identity as a child of God. Amen.*

As the Lord brings those areas of family sins to your mind, list them below. You will be specifically renouncing them later in this step.

1. _____

2. _____

3. _____

4. _____

In order to walk free from the sins of your ancestors and any curses and assignments targeted against you, read the following declaration and pray the following prayer out loud. Let the words come from your heart as you remember the authority you have in Christ Jesus.

Declaration

> *I here and now reject and disown all the sins of my ancestors. I specifically renounce the sins of (<u>name the areas of family sin the Lord revealed to you</u>). As one who has been delivered from the domain of darkness and placed into the kingdom of God's Son, I cancel out all demonic working that has been passed down to me from my family.*
>
> *As one who is crucified and raised with Jesus Christ and who sits with Him in heavenly places, I renounce all satanic assignments that are directed toward me and my ministry. I cancel out every curse that Satan and his workers have put on me. I announce to Satan and all his forces that Christ became a curse for me when He died for my sins on the cross.*
>
> *I reject any and every way in which Satan may claim ownership of me. I belong to the Lord Jesus Christ who purchased me with His own blood. I reject any blood sacrifices whereby Satan may claim ownership of me. I declare myself to be eternally and completely signed over and committed to the Lord Jesus Christ.*
>
> *By the authority that I have in Jesus Christ, I now command every enemy of the Lord Jesus Christ that is influencing me to leave my presence. I commit myself to my heavenly Father, to do His will from this day forward.*
>
> (See Galatians 3:13.)

Prayer

> *Dear heavenly Father, I come to You as Your child, purchased by the blood of the Lord Jesus Christ. You are the Lord*

of the universe and the Lord of my life. I submit my body to You as an instrument of righteousness, a living sacrifice, that I may glorify You in my body. I ask You to fill me with Your Holy Spirit to lead and empower me to know and do Your will. I commit myself to the renewing of my mind in order to prove that Your will is good, perfect, and acceptable for me. All this I do in the name and authority of the Lord Jesus Christ, amen.

Maintaining Your Freedom

Now that you have gone through these seven steps, you may find demonic influences attempting to gain control of your mind again days or even months later. One person shared that she heard a spirit say to her mind, "I'm back," two days after she had been set free. "No, you're not!" she proclaimed aloud. The attack stopped immediately.

The devil is attracted to sin like flies are attracted to garbage. Get rid of the garbage, and the flies will depart for smellier places. In the same way, walk in the truth, confessing all sin and forgiving those who hurt you, and the devil will have no place in your life to set up shop.

Realize that one victory does not mean the battles are over. After completing the steps, one happy girl asked, "Will I always be like this?" I told her that she would stay free as long as she remained in right relationship with God. "Even if you slip and fall," I encouraged her, "you know how to get right with God again."

One victim of incredible abuse shared this illustration:

> It's like being forced to play a game with an ugly stranger in my own home. I kept losing and wanted to quit, but the ugly stranger wouldn't let me. Finally I called the

> police (a higher authority), and they came and escorted
> the stranger out. He knocked on the door trying to
> regain entry, but this time I recognized his voice and
> didn't let him in.

What a beautiful illustration of gaining freedom in Christ! We call upon Jesus, the final and most powerful authority, and He escorts the powers of darkness out of our lives.

How to Maintain Your Freedom

Freedom must be maintained. We cannot emphasize that point enough. You have won a very important battle in an ongoing war. Freedom will remain yours as long as you keep choosing truth and standing firm in the strength of the Lord. If new memories should surface, or if you become aware of lies you have believed or other non-Christian experiences you have had, renounce them and choose the truth. If you realize that there are some other people you need to forgive, Step 3 will remind you of what to do. Most people have found it helpful to walk through the Steps to Freedom in Christ again. As you do, read the instructions carefully.

We recommend that you read the book *Stomping Out the Darkness* to strengthen your understanding of your identity in Christ. The *Bondage Breaker Youth Edition* will help you overcome spiritual problems. If you struggle with sexual bondage or desire to learn more about friendships and dating, we recommend *Purity Under Pressure.* We strongly suggest the following as well:

- *Get involved in a loving church youth group or Bible study* where you can be open and honest with other believers your age.

- *Study your Bible daily.* There are many great youth Bibles around for you to use. Begin to get into God's Word and memorize key verses. Remember, it is the truth that *sets* you free and it is the truth that *keeps* you free! You may want to say the "Statement of Truth" out loud daily and study the verses. (In addition, the youth devotionals *Extreme Faith, Reality Check,* and *Ultimate Love* have been developed especially to help you grow.)

- *Learn to take every thought captive to the obedience of Christ.* Assume responsibility for your thought life. Don't let your mind go passive. Reject all lies, choose to focus on the truth, and stand firm in your identity in Christ.

- *Don't drift away!* It is very easy to become lazy in your thoughts and slip back into old patterns of thinking. Share your struggles openly with a trusted friend who will pray for you.

- *Don't expect others to fight your battles for you.* They can't and they won't. Others can encourage you, but they can't think, pray, read the Bible, or choose the truth for you.

- *Commit yourself to daily prayer.* Prayer is dependence upon God. See appendix G for some suggested prayers you can pray often and with confidence.

Renew Your Mind in Christ

Continue to seek your identity and sense of worth through who you are in Christ. Renew your mind with the truth that your *acceptance, security,* and *significance* are in Christ alone. Meditate on the following truths daily, reading the entire list out loud, morning and evening, over the next few weeks.

In Christ

I Am Accepted

John 1:12	I am a child of God.
John 15:15	I am Jesus' chosen friend.
Romans 5:1	I am holy and acceptable to God (justified).
1 Corinthians 6:17	I am united to the Lord and am one spirit with Him.
1 Corinthians 6:19-20	I have been bought with a price. I belong to God.
1 Corinthians 12:27	I am a part of Christ's body—part of His family
Ephesians 1:1	I am a saint, a holy one.
Ephesians 1:5	I have been adopted as God's child.
Colossians 1:14	I have been bought back (redeemed) and forgiven of all my sins.
Colossians 2:10	I am complete.

I Am Secure

Romans 8:1-2	I am free forever from punishment.
Romans 8:28	I am sure all things work together for good.
Romans 8:31-34	I am free from any condemning charges against me.
Romans 8:35-39	I cannot be separated from the love of God.
Colossians 3:3	I am hidden with Christ in God.

Philippians 1:6	I am sure that the good work that God has started in me will be finished.
Ephesians 2:19	I am a citizen of heaven along with the rest of God's family.
Hebrews 4:16	I can find grace and mercy in times of need.
1 John 5:18	I am born of God, and the evil one cannot touch me.

I Am Significant

Matthew 5:13-14	I am salt and light for everyone around me.
John 15:1,5	I am part of the true vine, joined to Christ and able to produce lots of fruit.
John 15:16	I am hand-picked by Jesus to bear fruit.
Acts 1:8	I am a Spirit-empowered witness of Christ.
1 Corinthians 3:16	I am a temple where the Holy Spirit lives.
2 Corinthians 5:17-21	I am at peace with God and He has given me the work of making peace between Himself and other people.
2 Corinthians 6:1	I am God's co-worker.
Ephesians 2:6	I am seated with Christ in heaven.
Ephesians 2:10	I am God's building project, His hand-iwork, created to do His work.
Philippians 4:13	I am able to do all things through Christ who gives me strength!

APPENDIX A
TO THE STEPS TO FREEDOM IN CHRIST

Preparation for Taking Someone Through the Steps to Freedom

Before you start the Steps to Freedom, go over the events of your life so that you understand which areas might need to be dealt with. The following Confidential Spiritual Inventory can be used for that purpose.

Family History

- ❐ Religious background of parents and grandparents
- ❐ Your home life from childhood to the present
- ❐ Any history of physical or emotional problems in the family
- ❐ Adoption, foster care, guardians

Personal History

- ❐ *Spiritual journey.* Do you know if you are saved? If yes, how do you know you are saved? When did that happen?
- ❐ *Eating habits.* Do you make yourself vomit, take laxatives, or starve yourself to lose weight? Do you binge or eat uncontrollably?
- ❐ *Free Time.*
    - ❐ How many hours of TV do you watch a day?
    - ❐ What are your favorite TV shows?
    - ❐ How much time do you spend playing video or computer games each day?

❒ How much time do you spend listening to music per day?

❒ What kind of music do you listen to?

❒ How much time do you spend reading each day?

❒ What do you spend most of your time reading?

❒ Do you smoke? Chew tobacco? Drink alcohol?

❒ Do you use street drugs? If so, what kind?

❒ Prescription drugs? What for?

❒ Have you ever run away from home?

❒ Do you have trouble sleeping too little or too much?

❒ Do you experience frequent or recurring nightmares?

❒ Were you ever raped or abused sexually, physically, verbally, or emotionally?

❒ Do you suffer from distracting thoughts while in church, prayer, or Bible study?

Physical Life

(Check those that apply.)

❒ frequent headaches or migraines

❒ memory problems

❒ constant tiredness

❒ fainting spells or dizziness

❒ stomach problems

❒ allergies

Thought Life

(Check those that apply.)

❒ daydreaming or fantasy

❒ insecurity

❒ inferiority

❒ worry

❒ inadequacy

❒ self-hatred

❒ perfectionism

❒ doubts about salvation or God's love

❒ lust

❒ suicide

Emotional Life

(Check those that apply.)

❒ frustration

❒ fear of death

❒ anger

❒ fear of losing your mind

❒ anxiety

❒ fear of confusion

❒ depression

❒ fear of failure

❒ guilt

❒ fear of going to hell

❒ loneliness

❒ fear of the dark

❒ worthlessness

❒ fear of parents divorcing

❒ bitterness

APPENDIX B
TO THE STEPS TO FREEDOM IN CHRIST

Satanic Ritual Abuse Renunciations

If you have been involved in any satanic rituals or heavy occult activity, you need to say aloud the following special renunciations and affirmations.

Read across the next page, renouncing the first item in the column under "Domain of Darkness," and then affirming the first truth in the column under "Kingdom of Light." Continue down the entire list in that manner.

All satanic rituals, covenants (promises), and assignments must be specifically renounced as the Lord brings them to your mind. Some people who have been subjected to Satanic ritual abuse (SRA) develop multiple personalities (alters) in order to cope with their pain. In this case, you need someone who understands spiritual conflicts to help you maintain control and not be deceived into false memories. You can continue to walk through the Steps to Freedom in order to resolve all conflicts that you are aware of. Only Jesus can bind up the brokenhearted, set captives free, and make us whole.

Special Renunciations for Satanic Ritual Involvement

Domain of Darkness	*Kingdom of Light*
1. I renounce ever signing or having my name signed over to Satan.	1. I announce that my name is now written in the Lamb's Book of Life.
2. I renounce any ritual whereby I was wed to Satan.	2. I announce that I am part of the bride of Christ.
3. I renounce any and all covenants, agreements, or promises that I made to Satan.	3. I announce that I have made a new covenant with Jesus Christ alone that supersedes any previous agreements.
4. I renounce all satanic assignments for my life, including duties, marriage, and children.	4. I announce and commit myself to know and do only the will of God, and I accept only His guidance for my life.
5. I renounce all spirit guides assigned to me.	5. I announce and accept only the leading of the Holy Spirit.
6. I renounce any giving of my blood in the service of Satan.	6. I trust only in the shed blood of my Lord, Jesus Christ.
7. I renounce ever eating flesh or drinking blood in satanic worship.	7. By faith, I take Holy Communion, the body and blood of the Lord Jesus.
8. I renounce all guardians and satanist parents that were assigned to me.	8. I announce that God is my heavenly Father and the Holy Spirit is my guardian by whom I am sealed.
9. I renounce any baptism whereby I am identified with Satan.	9. I announce that I have been baptized into Christ Jesus and my identity is now in Him alone.
10. I renounce any sacrifice made on my behalf by which Satan may claim ownership of me.	10. I announce that only the sacrifice of Christ has any claim on me. I belong to Him. I have been purchased by the blood of the Lamb.

APPENDIX C
TO THE STEPS TO FREEDOM IN CHRIST

The Truth About Our Heavenly Father

Sometimes we are greatly hindered from walking by faith in our Father God because of lies that we have believed about Him. We are to have a healthy fear of God (awe of His holiness, power, and presence), but we are not to be afraid of Him. Romans 8:15 says, "You have not received a spirit of slavery leading to fear again, but you have received a spirit of adoption as sons by which we cry out, 'Abba Father!'" The following exercise will help break the chains of those lies and enable you to begin to experience that intimate "Abba, Father" relationship with Him.

Work your way down the list on the next page, one by one, left to right. Begin each point with the statement at the top of that list. Read through the list aloud.

The Truth About Our Heavenly Father

I renounce the lie that my Father God is...	*I joyfully accept the truth that my Father God is...*
1. distant and uninterested	1. intimate and involved (Psalm 139:1-8)
2. insensitive and uncaring	2. kind and compassionate (Psalm 103:8-14)
3. stern and demanding	3. accepting and filled with joy and love (Zephaniah 3:17; Romans 15:7)
4. passive and cold	4. warm and affectionate (Isaiah 40:11; Hosea 11:3-4)
5. absent or too busy for me	5. always with me and eager to be with me (Jeremiah 31:20; Ezekiel 34:11-16; Hebrews 13:5)
6. never satisfied with what I do; impatient, angry	6. patient and slow to anger (Exodus 34:6; 2 Peter 3:9)
7. mean, cruel, or abusive	7. loving, gentle, and protective of me (Psalm 18:2; Jeremiah 31:3; Isaiah 42:3)
8. trying to take all the fun out of life	8. trustworthy and wants to give me a full life; His will is good, perfect, and acceptable (Lamentations 3:22-23; John 10:10; Romans 12:1-2)
9. controlling or manipulative	9. full of grace and mercy; He gives me freedom to fail (Luke 15:11-16; Hebrews 4:15-16)
10. condemning or unforgiving	10. tenderhearted and forgiving; His heart and arms are always open to me (Psalm 130:1-4; Luke 15:17-24)
11. nit-picking, exacting, or perfectionistic	11. committed to my growth and proud of me as His growing child (Romans 8:28-29; 2 Corinthians 7:4; Hebrews 12:5-11)

I am the apple of His eye!
(Deuteronomy 32:10 NIV)

Appendix D
to the Steps to Freedom in Christ

Dealing with Fears

A central part of walking in the truth and rejecting deception is to deal with the fears that plague our lives. First Peter 5:8 says that our enemy, the devil, prowls around like a roaring lion, seeking people to devour. Just as a lion's roar strikes terror into the hearts of those who hear it, so Satan uses fear to try to paralyze Christians. His intimidation tactics are designed to rob us of faith in God and to drive us to try to get our needs met through the world or the flesh.

Fear weakens us, causes us to be self-centered, and clouds our minds so that all we can think about is the thing that frightens us. But fear can only control us if we let it.

God, however, does not want us to be mastered by anything, including fear (1 Corinthians 6:12). Jesus Christ is to be our only Master (2 Timothy 2:21; John 13:13). In order to begin to experience freedom from the bondage of fear and to be able to walk by faith in God, pray the following prayer from your heart.

> *Dear heavenly Father, I confess to You that I have listened to the devil's roar and have allowed fear to master me. I have not always walked by faith in You but instead have focused on my feelings and circumstances. I thank You for forgiving me for my unbelief.*
>
> *Right now I renounce the spirit of fear and affirm the truth that You have not given me a spirit of fear, but of power, love, and a sound mind. Lord, please reveal to my mind now all the fears that have been controlling me so that I can renounce them and be free to walk by faith in You. I*

thank You for the freedom You give me to walk by faith and not by fear. In Jesus' powerful name I pray, amen.

(See 2 Corinthians 4:16-18; 5:7; 2 Timothy 1:7.)

The following list may help you to recognize some of the fears that the devil has used to keep you from walking by faith. Check the ones that apply to your life. Write down any others that the Spirit of God brings to your mind. Then, one by one, renounce those fears aloud, using the suggested renunciation below.

- ❏ Fear of death
- ❏ Fear of being a hopeless case
- ❏ Fear of Satan
- ❏ Fear of losing my salvation
- ❏ Fear of failure
- ❏ Fear of having committed the unpardonable sin
- ❏ Fear of rejection by people
- ❏ Fear of disapproval
- ❏ Fear of not being loved by God
- ❏ Fear of financial problems
- ❏ Fear of embarrassment
- ❏ Fear of never getting married
- ❏ Fear of being victimized
- ❏ Fear of becoming homosexual
- ❏ Fear of marriage
- ❏ Fear of the death of a loved one
- ❏ Fear of divorce
- ❏ Fear of going crazy

❒ Fear of pain
❒ Fear of never being able to love or be loved by anyone
❒ Other specific fears that come to mind now:

I renounce (<u>name the fear</u>) because God has not given me a spirit of fear. I choose to live by faith in the God who has promised to protect me and meet all my needs as I walk by faith in Him.

(See Psalm 27:1; Matthew 6:33-34.)

After you have finished renouncing all the specific fears that you have allowed to control you, pray the following prayer from your heart:

Dear heavenly Father, I thank You that You are trustworthy. I choose to believe You even when my feelings and circumstances tell me to fear. You have told me not to fear, for You are with me; not to anxiously look about me, for You are my God. You will strengthen me, help me, and surely uphold me with Your righteous right hand. I pray this with faith in the name of Jesus, my Master, amen.

(See Isaiah 41:10.)

Appendix E
to the Steps to Freedom in Christ

Dealing with Prejudice and Bigotry

Pride is the original sin of Lucifer. It sets one person or group against another. Satan's strategy is always to divide and conquer, but God has given us a ministry of reconciliation (2 Corinthians 5:19). Take a look for a moment at the work of Christ in breaking down the long-standing barrier of racial prejudice between Jews and Gentiles:

> For [Christ] is our peace, who has made the two one and destroyed the barrier, the dividing wall of hostility, by abolishing in his flesh the law with its commandments and regulations. His purpose was to create in himself one new man out of the two, thus making peace, and in this one body to reconcile both of them to God through the cross, by which he put to death their hostility. He came and preached peace to you who were far away and peace to those who were near. For through him we both have access to the Father by one Spirit (Ephesians 2:14-18 NIV).

Many times we deny that there is prejudice or bigotry in our hearts, yet "nothing in all creation is hidden from God's sight. Everything is uncovered and laid bare before the eyes of him to whom we must give account" (Hebrews 4:13 NIV). The following prayer asks God to shine His light upon your heart and reveal any area of proud prejudice:

> *Dear heavenly Father, I know that You love all people equally and that You do not play favorites. You accept people from every nation who fear You and do what is right. You do not judge them based on skin color, race, how much money they*

have, ethnic background, gender, what church they go to, or any other worldly matter.

I confess that I have too often prejudged others or thought of myself as superior because of these things. I have not always been a minister of reconciliation, but have promoted division through my attitudes, words, and deeds. I repent of all hateful bigotry and proud prejudice, and I ask you, Lord, to now show to my mind all the ways this kind of pride has polluted my heart and mind. In Jesus' name, amen.

(See Acts 10:34; 2 Corinthians 5:16)

For each area of prejudice, superiority, or bigotry that the Lord brings to mind, pray the following prayer out loud from your heart:

I confess and renounce the prideful sin of prejudice against (name the group). I thank You for Your forgiveness, Lord, and ask now that You would change my heart and make me a loving agent of reconciliation with (name the group). In Jesus' name, amen.

APPENDIX F
TO THE STEPS TO FREEDOM IN CHRIST

Special Prayers for Specific Needs

Abortion

Note to men: Just as mothers are called to be responsible for the life that God has entrusted to them, so too the father shares in this responsibility. If you have failed to fulfill your role as a father or a mother, pray the following prayer:

> *Lord, I confess that I was not a proper guardian and keeper of the life You entrusted to me, and I admit that as sin. I choose to accept Your forgiveness, and I now commit that child to You for Your care for all eternity. In Jesus' name, amen.*

Drivenness and Perfectionism

> *Lord, I renounce the lie that my self-worth is dependent on my ability to perform. I announce the truth that my identity and sense of worth is found in who I am as your child. I renounce seeking the approval and acceptance of other people, and I choose to believe that I am already approved and accepted in Christ because of His death and resurrection for me. I choose to believe the truth that I have been saved, not by deeds that I have done, but according to Your mercy.*
>
> *I choose to believe that I am no longer under the curse of the law because Jesus became a curse for me. I receive the free gift of life in Christ, and I choose to abide in Him. I renounce striving for perfection by living under the law. By your grace, heavenly Father, I choose from this day forward to walk by faith according to what You said is true by the power of the Holy Spirit. In Jesus' name, amen.*

Eating Disorders or Cutting Yourself

Lord, I renounce the lie that my value as a person is dependent upon my physical beauty, my weight, or my size. I renounce cutting myself, vomiting, using laxatives, or starving myself as a means of cleansing myself of evil or altering my appearance. I announce that only the blood of the Lord Jesus Christ cleanses me from sin.

I accept the reality that there may be sin present in me because of the lies I have believed and because of the wrongful use of my body, but I renounce the lie that I am evil or that any part of my body is evil. My body is the temple of the Holy Spirit, and I belong to God. I am totally accepted by God in Christ—just as I am. In Jesus' name, amen.

Homosexuality

Lord, I renounce the lie that You have created me or anyone else to be homosexual, and I declare that You created me to be a man (or a woman). I renounce all homosexual thoughts, urges, or drives, as well as any bondage of Satan, that have perverted my relationships with others. I announce that I am free to relate to the opposite sex and my own sex in the way that You have intended. In Jesus' name, amen.

Substance Abuse

Lord, I now confess that I have misused substances (alcohol, tobacco, food, prescription or street drugs) for the purpose of pleasure, to escape reality, or to cope with difficult problems. I confess that I have abused my body and programmed my mind in a harmful way. I have not allowed Your Holy Spirit to guide me.

I ask Your forgiveness, and I reject any satanic connection or influence in my life because of my misuse of chemicals or food. I cast my cares onto Christ, who loves me. I commit myself to no longer give in to substance abuse, but instead to allow the Holy Spirit to lead and empower me. In Jesus' name, amen.

Suicidal Tendencies

Lord, I renounce suicidal thoughts and any attempts I may have made to take my own life or in any way injure myself. I renounce the lie that life is hopeless and that I can find peace and freedom by taking my own life. Satan is a thief, and he comes to steal, kill, and destroy. I choose life in Christ, who said He came to give me life and give it to the full. I choose to accept Your forgiveness and believe that there is always hope in Christ. In Jesus' name, amen.

After you have confessed all known sin, say,

I now confess these sins to You and claim my forgiveness and cleansing through the blood of the Lord Jesus Christ. I cancel out all ground that evil spirits have gained through my willful involvement in sin. I ask this in the wonderful name of my Lord and Savior, Jesus Christ, amen.

APPENDIX G
TO THE STEPS TO FREEDOM IN CHRIST

Daily Prayer

Bedtime Prayer

Prayer for Cleansing Room, Apartment, or Home

Daily Prayer

Dear heavenly Father, I honor You as my Lord. I know that You are always present with me. You are the only all-powerful and the only wise God. You are kind and loving in all Your ways. I love You, and I thank You that I am united with Christ and spiritually alive in Him. I choose not to love the world, and I crucify the flesh and all its passions.

I thank You for the life that I now have in Christ, and I ask You to fill me and guide me with Your Holy Spirit so I may live my life free from sin. I declare my dependence upon You. I take my stand against Satan and all his lying ways. I choose to believe the truth, and I refuse to be discouraged. You are the God of all hope, and I am confident that You will meet my needs as I seek to live according to Your Word. I express with confidence that I can live a responsible life through Christ, who strengthens me.

I now take my stand against Satan and command him and all his evil spirits to depart from me. I put on the whole armor of God. I submit my body as a living sacrifice and renew my mind by Your living Word in order that I may prove that your will is good, acceptable, and perfect. I ask these things in the powerful and precious name of my Lord and Savior, Jesus Christ, amen.

Bedtime Prayer

Thank you, Lord, that you have brought me into Your family and have blessed me with every spiritual blessing in the heavenly realms in Christ. Thank you, too, for providing this time of renewal through sleep. I accept it as part of Your perfect plan for Your children, and I trust You to guard my mind and my body during sleep.

Just as I have thought about You and Your truth during the day, I choose to let those thoughts continue in my mind while I am asleep. I commit myself to You for Your protection from every attempt of Satan or his demons to attack me during the night. I commit myself to You as my rock, my fortress, and my resting place. I pray in the strong name of the Lord Jesus Christ, amen.

Prayer for Cleansing Home, Apartment, or Room

After removing and destroying all articles of false worship (crystals, good-luck charms, occultic objects, games, and so on), pray out loud in your sleeping area,

Thank you, heavenly Father, for a place to live and be renewed by sleep. I ask You to set aside my room (or my portion of room) as a place of safety for me. I renounce any worship given to false gods or spirits by other occupants, and I renounce any claim to this room (space) by Satan, based on what people have done here or what I have done in the past.

On the basis of my position as a child of God and a joint heir with Christ, who has all the authority in heaven and on earth, I command all evil spirits to leave this place and never to return. I ask You, heavenly Father, to appoint guardian angels to protect me while I live here. I pray this in the name of the Lord Jesus Christ, amen.

Notes

Chapter 1—A World Living in Fear

1. Adapted from *Time* magazine, September 24, 2001, pp. 64-65; and *People* magazine, September 24, 2001.

2. "Anxiety Disorders Most Common U.S. Mental Illness," National Institute of Mental Health, October 1996, p. 1.

Chapter 2—Fearful Heart

1. Jim Burns, *No Compromise* (Ventura, CA: Regal Books, 2002), pp. 10-11. Used by Permission.

2. Max Lucado, *When Christ Comes* (Nashville, TN: Word Publishing, 1999), pp. 21-22.

3. Jim Burns and Greg McKinnon, *Stories and Quotes You Can Hang Your Message On* (Ventura, CA: Gospel Light, 1997), p. 169.

Chapter 3—Overcoming the Fear of Man

1. Bill Bright, *Witnessing Without Fear* (San Bernardino, CA: Here's Life Publishers, Inc., 1987), p. 13.

2. Bright, pp. 54-65.

3. Adapted from Bright, pp. 59-61.

4. Adapted and condensed from Misty Bernall, *She Said Yes* (Nashville, TN: Word Publishers, 1999), pp. 1-34.

5. Adapted and condensed from Angus Kinnear, *Against the Tide: Watchman Nee* (Fort Washington, PA: Christian Literature Crusade, Inc., 1992); as contained in Robert J. Morgan, *More Real Stories for the Soul* (Nashville, TN: Thomas Nelson Publishers, 2000), pp. 94-98.

Chapter 4—Overcoming the Fear of Death

1. As cited in *USA Weekend*, August 22-24, 1997, p. 6.

2. Ibid., p. 5.

3. Ibid.

4. Nickelodeon/Yankelovich *Youth Monitor*, as quoted in *USA Today*, October 6, 1998, p. D1.

5. Cheryl Wetzstein, "Preteens have great trust in parents," *The Washington Times*, May 16, 1995, p. A2.

6. Kaiser Permanente and Children Now poll, as cited in Alison Bell, "The Fear Factor," *Teen* magazine, April 1997, p. 6.

7. Ibid.

8. Bonnie Crandall, *Panic Buster* (Jamestown, NY: Hatch Creek Publishing, 1995), p.14.

9. Crandall, p.14.

Chapter 5—Overcoming the Fear of Failure

1. Adapted from "Schilling Works Hard to Reach New Heights," *USA Today*, August 28, 2002, section 2-C.

2. Susan Jeffers, *Feel the Fear and Do It Anyway* (New York: Fawcett Columbine, 1987), p. 4.

3. Jeffers, pp. 22, 23.

4. Kent Keith, *Anyway: The Paradoxical Commandments* (New York: Putnam Publishing Group, 2002).

Chapter 6—Overcoming Panic Attacks

1. David G. Benner, *Baker Encyclopedia of Psychology* (Grand Rapids, MI: Baker Book House, 1990), p. 786.

2. "Answers to Your Questions About Panic Disorder," American Psychological Association, p. 1.

3. "Answers to Your Questions."

4. "Panic Disorder," American Psychiatric Association, 1997, p. 2.

5. "Panic Disorder," National Anxiety Foundation, p. 2.

6. R. Reid Wilson, Ph.D., *Don't Panic* (New York: HarperCollins Publishers, 1996), p. 32.

7. Ibid., p. 34.

Chapter 7—Breaking Strongholds of Fear

1. The "Phobic Finder" was originally contained in Neil Anderson, *Walking in the Light* (Nashville, TN: Thomas Nelson, 1992), p. 68.

2. Adapted from Edmund J. Bourne, *The Anxiety and Phobia Workbook* (Oakland, CA: New Harbinger Publications, Inc., 1998), pp. 152-53.

Chapter 9—The Fear that Destroys All Other Fears

1. *The New Bible Dictionary* (Grand Rapids, MI: Wm. B. Eerdmans Publishing Co., 1977), "Fear."

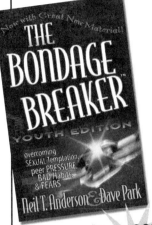

Other Books by Neil Anderson and Dave Park

The Bondage Breaker Youth Edition
The Bondage Breaker Youth Edition Study Guide
Stomping Out the Darkness
Stomping Out the Darkness Study Guide
Busting Free Youth Curriculum
Busting Free Video Series

FREEDOM IN CHRIST 4 TEENS

Awesome God
by Neil Anderson and Rich Miller

Extreme Faith
by Neil Anderson and Dave Park

Purity Under Pressure
by Neil Anderson and Dave Park

Reality Check
by Neil Anderson and Rich Miller

Righteous Pursuit
by Neil Anderson and Dave Park

Ultimate Love
by Neil Anderson and Rich Miller

FREEDOM IN CHRIST
ADULT AND STUDENT CONFERENCES

Stomping Out the Darkness
for high school and junior high students

The Seduction of Our Teens
Parent seminar will help parents make
a lasting spiritual impact at home

Setting Your Youth Free
Equips adults to have a powerful
freedom ministry in the church

Purity Under Pressure
Helps students overcome sexual pressures
and establish godly relationships

Total Abandon
This prayer conference will help you hear
the voice of God and follow His leading

FREEDOM IN CHRIST YOUTH MINISTRIES

A Resource Ministry to Youth and the Church
Leading Teens, Parents, and Youth Leaders
to a Message of Freedom in Christ

For more information about having a
Freedom in Christ Ministries event in your area,
call, write, or e-mail:

Freedom in Christ Youth Ministries
9051 Executive Park Dr., #503
Knoxville, TN 37923

Phone: 865-342-4000, ext. 105
Fax: 865-342-4001
E-mail: davepark@ficm.org
Website: www.ficyouth.com